1147 RANDOM AND INTERESTING, FUN FACT EVERYONE SHOULD KNOW

JAMIE BANTHER

COPYRIGHT © 2023

ISBN : 9789693292633

TABLE OF CONTENTS

INTRODUCTION 4

THE MOST BIZARRE THINGS 6

INTERESTING FACTS ABOUT FOOD......................12

CHARMING FACTS ABOUT SPORT 19

UNBELIEVABLE CULTURE 23

FASCINATING MOVIE FACTS 30

MOVIES WITH THE GREATEST SOUNDTRACKS 35

FACTS ABOUT THE NOTORIOUS CRIME WORLD 40

MEDICAL PROCEDURES & ABNORMALITIES 46

NOTEWORTHY HISTORICAL DATES 52

UNBELIEVABLE HOUSEHOLD HACKS FOR CLEANING AND ORGANIZING... 74

CAPTIVATING FACTS ABOUT SCIENCE 92

SCIENTISTS THAT DIED OR GOT INJURED BY THEIR EXPERIMENTS 94

MESMERIZING FACTS ABOUT MUSIC..............................98

STRANGE ANIMAL FACTS 104

INTRIGUING MISCELLANEOUS FACTS 119

Conclusion 163

3

INTRODUCTION

Hey there, explorer of the extraordinary! You've just crash-landed into the fun-filled universe of "Facts Galore: The Ultimate Brain Candy for the Curiously Keen"! Buckle up because you're about to embark on an epic adventure through the twisted corridors of human knowledge.

Think of this book as your golden ticket to the fact factory where the truth is stranger than fiction. Whether you're the kind of person who marvels at the thought of sharks being older than trees or you ponder over how a single spaghetti strand is called "spaghetto," we've got your back. This is not just any fact book; it's a rollercoaster ride through the wild, wild world we inhabit.

Inside, you'll unearth secrets from the past, marvel at nature's wonders, cheer for sports oddities, savor delicious foodie facts, gasp at movie magic, get enlightened on the enigmas of religion, and dance to the beat of musical trivia. You'll even rub elbows with celebrities, tiptoe through political tidbits, jam out to musical marvels, and solve crimes with a mere flip of the page!

We've scoured the globe, dived into history, and soared through the stars to gather a treasure trove of knowledge nuggets. And guess what? We've peppered the journey with illustrations that paint a thousand words and bring our stories to life.

This isn't just any compilation—it's a celebration of curiosity, a testament to the tales and truths that make our world such a wacky and wonderful place. Each fact is a story, every chapter a gateway to awe, and with 1147 mesmerizing truths, you're set for a non-stop thrill ride of enlightenment. 🎉

So what are you waiting for? Dive into this mind-boggling expedition of awe-inspiring facts. You're not weird for loving the quirky and the quizzical—you're about to become the most interesting person in the room. Welcome aboard, fact-finder. Let's make some history together with brain-bursting facts that'll knock your socks off! 💬 💥 🌍

THE MOST BIZARRE THINGS

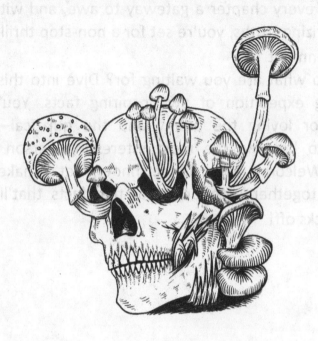

1. Just when I thought I have heard the most cringing thing, then coprophagia creeps in. This is a strong desire to eat your feces or that of others.

2. Doctor Julien Offray De La Mettrie ate himself to death. Well ironically! Julien died at a party hosted by a man he cured where he ate his last plates of truffle pâté.

3. I recommend bird poop for your facials. The use of bird poop for facial treatment was an ancient Japanese beauty secret called "uguisu no fun" found in nightingales.

4. Ever heard of people who are alive but think they are dead? This disorder is called Cotard delusion, named after Jules Cotard in 1880.

5. In your wildest dream, you'd never imagine that pure wolf urine would be sold on Amazon. Many have said it helps chase uninvited creatures at home.

6. Elizabeth Short was nicknamed "The Black Dahlia" after the movie "The Blue Dahlia." Investigators found her body cut in two parts in a parking lot in Los Angeles.

7. Meet Jean Baptista dos Santos born Dos Santos had a third leg, 2 working penises, 3 scrota, & the 2 external ones had 1 testis.

8. Way back in Persia, criminals are killed in the most inhumane manner called Scaphism. What a way to die!

9. When did humans graduate from normal meals to eating glasses? Glass eating is a very serious sickness called Hyalophagia.

10. There is a building in America that contains various kinds of vibrators. It is called Antique Vibrator Museum.

11. Who doesn't like new things or new experiences? Well, Neophobic people don't!

12. With all the advancement in tech which has made life more bearable, some people wish we never had it; they are suffering from technophobia.

13. One time a 23-foot-long reticulated python swallowed an Indonesian woman who had gone missing. They cut the python open and she was intact.

14. Northern California was disturbed by a Zodiac serial killer for months. He killed five people, maimed two, sent clues to the police, and wasn't caught.

15. Dr. John's Pee bottle has saved so many from embarrassment today. If you are set to take a drug test and you know you'd fail, use this synthetic pee.

16. Empedocles fell into an active volcano at Mount Etna in Sicily and said he'll return as a god. Regrettably, his followers saw his folly after finding a pair of his sandals.

17. In Honduras, the murder rate is so great that some cities have started giving a program for free funerals.

18. Tragedy struck as Aeschylus died instantly after an eagle dropped a tortoise on his head thinking it was an egg.

19. Matthew McConaughey was afflicted by a food fetish and had to stop eating so as not to get too sexually aroused by the food.

20. The safesex suit looks like a space suit that protects one from disease and joy during sexual intercourse.

21. Frederik Ruysch's collection had animals with an abnormal sum of body parts legs, and live freaks he put on display in 1719.

22. There is a genetic mutation that afflicts only four known extended families called Adermatoglyphia.

23. Seen real-life incest before? Patrick Stuebing and Susan Karolewski fell in love, got married, and had kids. When they discovered they were related they chose to go to jail rather than stop the practice.

24. Tibetan Buddhists bury their dead using the Sky burial method where the bones of the dead are crushed with a hammer and mallets till it is powdery. Then it is mixed with tea, barley flour, and yak butter and given to vultures.

25. Another very painful method of execution is flaying. It is the removal of an individual's skin from

the body while they are still alive, with a very sharp knife to keep the skin intact.

26. The beauty industry has fruitfully made synthetic snake venom out of the thousands of milked snakes at the snake farm in Brazil.

27. Blanche Dumas was born with a third leg, 4 breasts & 2 vaginas.

28. Jack the Ripper started in 1888 in London and his targets were prostitutes around the poor Whitechapel environ.

29. Paul Lovell was tried for bestiality in 2013, for sleeping with a sheep. He said he had sex with a sheep when a cow turned him down for fellatio.

30. A taxi man mistakenly knocked down and killed a young man riding a moped. A year later, the same taxi, killed the brother of the man he killed a year ago, and strangely the taxi carried the same passenger as the last time.

31. Karma they say is a *****! Eleazar Maccabeus died at the hands of the elephant he killed during the battle of Beth-Zechariah.

32. Ever heard of human cats? Some humans believe they are cats. It is a mental condition called

Galeanthropy which is displayed in the embracing of catlike habits.

33. Do you want shiny and smooth hair? Then I've got the best remedy for you – "Bull semen." Eww right! Well, if you are a sucker for healthy hair, know that bull semen holds a great source of concentrated protein.

34. In 1996, Sharon Lopatka died to fulfill her long wished sexual fantasy at the hands of Robert Frederick Glass who gave her deadly sexual gratification.

35. One time a Chinese family adopted what they felt was a Tibetan mastiff but it became an Asiatic black bear instead.

36. Turkey's Ulke TV reported that a driver of a Range Rover Sport traveling from Karakoy to Eminonu got on the tramway and got stuck.

37. A dozen camels were eliminated from a camel beauty competition for receiving Botox injections to make them more attractive in Saudi Arabia.

INTERESTING FACTS ABOUT FOOD

38. Would you drink hot chocolate that has chilies and corn in it? Well, that was the ideal hot chocolate drink for ancient Mayans.

39. Did you know that the very tasty red food coloring we love to add to our meals is derived from thousands of dead bugs? Yes! Cochineal bugs to be precise. It is also used to dye clothes.

40. I love a perfect combo, don't you too? Brazil has a healthy soup that keeps you full for a long and it's also an aphrodisiac called Piranha soup.

41. When I thought a meal covered in gold was the most expensive food item in the world, then Beluga caviar (fish roe eggs) comes to claim the prize.

42. Put brown frogs in milk to keep them fresh. Yes, this was a common practice in Russia and Finn before refrigerators came.

43. Did you know that 7-Up was formerly medicinal and was invented in 1920? It had lithium which helped in managing patients with bipolar disorder.

44. Harry Burt the candy-maker in Youngstown, Ohio made the first "ice cream on a stick" in 1920.

45. Instant noodles are said to be the greatest Japanese invention of the 20th century!

46. Netflix and chill with a cup of butter tea. Butter tea is a popular drink in Tibet made of salt, yak butter, and tea. Make a cup and thank me much later.

47. Chef Josh Niland's creation is the fish turducken. It is made with yellowfin tuna loin, covered in a cod fillet, and then wrapped in a huge tail-on ocean trout fillet.

48. Ever heard of the saying that the older a wine stays, the richer the taste? Meet the world's oldest chocolates from King Edward VII's coronation from 1902, sitting pretty at the St Andrews Preservation Trust Museum.

49. West Africa has a Miracle Berry that makes sour foods taste sweet.

50. Bakeapple is derived from the French word "Baie Qu'Appelle?" meaning "What's this berry called?"

51. Allura red AC is created from coal tar to serve as red food coloring, to replace amaranth which has more harmful substances.

52. The oldest recipe for ice cream was whale feces or ambergreece/ambergris, from way back in the 1660s.

53. Wondering what the approved fifth taste is? It's called Umami – It is a savory flavor caused by glutamate, an amino acid.

54. We have Thomas Jefferson to thank for making mac and cheese famous in America.

55. John Martin created the Moscow mule drink when he struggled to sell his vodka.

56. Will you be trying out bird's nest in your next meal? China uses Cave Swifts nests to make a great delicacy and it's very expensive.

57. It's a mystery that no one knows who invented donuts or what period in life they began to circulate.

58. Every strawberry is pregnant! The "seeds" outside the strawberry are not seeds but ovaries named achenes that hold a single fruit with a separate seed inside it. Just WOW!

59. Who is the world found beaver anal juice tastes fabulous with raspberries? This juice is used for other foodstuffs but mostly raspberries. It is found in cigarettes and chewing gum.

60. The management of KFC changed its name because they felt "fried" in their name had negative effects. Today they are back to saying their name out in full.

61. Iceland has puffins as their local delicacy. It's either grilled, smoked, or boiled.

62. Honey is the only food that doesn't spoil.

63. Want to know how to spot an egg that has gone bad? Put it in a bowl of water, if the egg doesn't float, then it is safe for consumption. But if the egg floats, then throw it away.

64. Did you know that a tea tree cannot be transplanted? In a Chinese wedding, tea represents love, loyalty, and a happily married life due to the significance of the tea tree that grows and sprouts from a seed.

65. Gold isn't a famous jewelry product anymore. It is now an additive, typically for decorative purposes as a gold leaf. It is commonly used in a German liqueur called Goldwasser (Goldwater) and it's not harmful to the body.

66. Meet the world's most pampered cattle who are fed beer and grain. These black Tajima-ushi breeds of Wagyu cattle are the most-tender and fatty beef called Kobe Beef.

67. Who would believe that Ice cream originated in China in 3000 BC? The recipe was made up of rice, milk, and snow.

68. In Newfoundland, there is a berry called a bakeapple.

69. Cigarettes are now used to make food!

70. Osteria Francescana was voted one of the world's best restaurants, it has a menu item called 'the crunchy part of the lasagna'.

71. The first known recipe for macaroni & cheese dates back to 14th-century England.

72. Rice is one of the most water-intensive crops to cultivate, it needs close to 2,500 liters per kilogram.

73. Wondering why you are addicted to vanilla? It is because of the catecholamines and adrenalin that are released in your body after taking natural vanilla, which is said to be addictive.

74. Research says that strawberry ice cream, strawberry flavors, perfumes, and cigarettes taste better with the addition of mammal poop. The ingredient in poop responsible for this is called "skatole".

75. Will you love a cup of animal fat for breakfast? The nauseating feeling is out of this world! Well, McDonald's shakes are created out of reconstituted fats from different animal fat.

76. I bet you didn't know that apples, onions, and potatoes have the same taste. Well, that's only possible when you have your nose plugged in while eating them!

77. Lovers of chocolate-chip cookies, meet – Ruth Wakefield, the real originator of the chocolate-chip cookie.

78. The stickers on fruits are harmless because the glue used is food grade.

79. Saffron is the most expensive spice in the globe. It is worth over $2,000 per pound, it is handpicked, and takes so much to get just an ounce of its spice.

80. Brain freeze was coined by 7-11 to describe the painful feeling one experiences when one drinks a Slurpee too fast.

81. Caffeine extracted from coffee beans is sold as rough caffeine to refiners and the pure caffeine is sold to soft drink makers like Pepsi and Coca-Cola.

82. Gather round lets meet the strangest and most amazing cheese ever – called Halloumi common in Cyprus.

83. Ketchup was formerly a fish sauce that originated from the orient!

84. A legend to many, meet soccer star Cristiano Ronaldo who didn't get any tattoos on his body just so he can continue donating blood!

85. Can you believe that the Argentine Football Association put out a publication on practical ways to seduce Russian women? Before the 2018 World Cup, a cultural manual containing that info circulated to Argentina.

86. Baseball player the great Ichiro Suzuki learned Spanish so he could trash talk his opponents during games.

87. Sex doll for a mannequin? LOL! FC Seoul a South Korean soccer team was fined 100 million Korean won for showing sex dolls in place of mannequins in their stand after the aftermath of the coronavirus.

88. In the movie "The Program" there's a scene where football players are laid in the middle of the highway to show they have nerves of steel as vehicles dodged them.

89. Far back in 1812, St. Andrews had rules of golf that were uncommon like; if your ball hits your opponent or their caddy, then they have lost the hole.

90. Only Grigori Perelman has cracked one of the seven Millennium Prize Problems. After resolving the Poincaré conjecture Perelman, he was offered both Field's Medal and $1 million prize money, but he rejected both!

91. Do you know where the term 'Tall Boy' originated from? Carnival artist Peter Minshall created it for the 1996 Olympic Games in Atlanta.

92. Athletes on wheelchairs love to have injuries in the lower part of their bodies before a game because it

increases BP called 'Boosting'. This act has been banned since 1994.

93. Did you know that the average energy spent in the ladies' Wimbledon tennis last match, can keep an iPhone powered for over a year? It's up to 1.56kWh.

94. The great Kobe Bryant missed the most shots in NBA history (14,481). But, he averaged 25.4 points each game throughout his career, shot 45.3%, and made 33% of his entire career three-pointers.

95. Muhammad Alias a child was refused an autograph by his boxing idol, Sugar Ray Robinson.

96. Experts say we burn more calories when we take a set of stairs each step at a time and not two steps per time.

97. Meet Philip Noel-Baker; the British politician who won an Olympic medal (silver in the 1500m) and a Nobel Peace Prize. He is the only one who has won this magnitude of prize ever in history.

98. Sean Connery was offered to play for Manchester United but decided to decline it and move on to the film industry.

99. The normal range of heart rate for many people is 60 - 72 BPM, but Miguel Induráin – a retired Spanish cyclist had a resting heart rate of 28 BPM.

100.   A huge turnaround took place in Table Tennis in 1937. The table tennis federation voted in 2000 to raise the diameter of the ping pong ball from 38mm to 40mm to make it simpler to learn and make the sport better for TV.

101.   In 2000, Spain's Paralympic basketball team was told to return their gold medals won in Sydney when the players had to have no disability.

102.   The squash player from Pakistan, Jahangir Khan played 555 serial squash matches, keeping an unbeaten run the entire time in 5 years.

103.   The only national team that has never lost a match against Brazil is the Norway national soccer team which has won two matches against Brazil and tied two.

104.   Next time anyone wrongs you, demand a public apology the way the Japanese culture does. In Japan, shaving your head is a popular form of public apology.

105.   Wouldn't you have loved to be baptized with cider? Well, in 14th century England, children were baptized with cider as this was cleaner than water.

106.   The Ottoman Empire was big on keeping their royal dynasty and evading a war of succession. Male heirs are locked in a section of the Imperial palace if they succeed the throne called Kafes also known as "the cage."

107.   The "fat Buddha" statue is not Siddhārtha Gautama, or "Buddha", but a different Chinese deity called Budai.

108.   The world's largest gathering of over 60 million people in attendance is the Kumbh Mela also known as Grand Pitcher Festival. Kumbh Mela is a big Hindu religious festival that holds every 12 years in India.

109.   El Colacho is the weirdest Spanish festival that began in 1620. It is the art of jumping over babies by adult men of the Castrillo de Murcia

village. This is a form of baptism carried out during the feast of Corpus Christi.

110.   If you want to improve in linguistics, learn from the people of Papua New Guinea. They are the most linguistically diverse nation in the world and has 851 languages.

111.   Thailand has a festival to appreciate their monkeys a Monkey Buffet Festival.

112.   Who would have thought that fireworks were first created to bring about prolonged life/immortality? This is an old Chinese quest dating way back to the 9th century.

113.   The custom of firing guns as a salute was initially a sign of peaceful intentions

114.   In ancient South America, babies wore burial head coverings created from the skulls of other children.

115.   Ever heard of a gathering of the sufferers of near-death episodes? People of Las Nieves Spain gather to celebrate Mass in a celebration of Fiesta De Santa Marta De Ribarteme, the patron saint of resurrection.

116.   Kobe Beef is produced only in Hyōgo Prefecture in Japan.

117.   Human composting became another legal option asides from cremation and burying in Washington State on May 1, 2020.

118.   Denmark has a beautiful and rich tradition called "Organic Day" celebrated by millions of people in April.

119.   Cleveland Indians formerly had a "10-cent beer night" that ends in the crowd rioting and attacking the players and umpires.

120.   Japan has the finest female pearl divers popularly called Ama or Uminchu. They begin to dive from age 12-13 and are very active till their 70s. The Ama are dressed in wetsuits and a traditional headscarf.

121.   The annual Goose clubbing festival by Germans is a cruel activity. This act has a goose tied at its feet against a post and local German clubs the goose till its head goes off. It's common in Spain and called Antzar Eguna.

122.   In the Republic of Tajikistan, birthdays aren't celebrated in the public except with close family.

123.   The sacrifice of a cucumber in place of an Ox is a better way to celebrate a festival. The people of Nilotic, Dinka, Nuer, and Atout of South Sudan.

124. Uganda is the home of mountain gorillas. It has over half of the world's full population of mountain gorillas which numbers 400 mountain gorillas.

125. Why the head-shaping practice is done is still uncertain to date. Dating back to over 14,000 years ago, ancient Chinese carried out head-shaping by taking young children's skulls to make a long and oval shape.

126. Don't you just want to be indigenes of Mexico, Belgium, Germany, and Austria? They don't give extra time to sentenced criminals who try to escape prison, they believe its human nature to desire to escape.

127. Yearly, a giant penis statue is displayed in Kawasaki Japan every spring to celebrate the Shinto fertility festival called Kanamara Matsuri (The Steel Phallus). Prostitutes believed it reeds them off sexually transmitted ailments.

128. China has received first place in achieving ways to make dog owners more responsible. Losing 12 points will rid the owners of their dogs, till the test is passed.

129.   In Mexico, the Tarahumara group of Native Americans are skillful to run 200 miles in one session and hunt by chasing their prey to death.

130.   Ever heard of incurring severe bodily pain just to draw blessings from your god? This is what the Hindus celebrated called Thaipusam Thaipusam. Celebrated commonly by Tamils at the start of a new year.

131.   In the past, a slice of bread is worth $1 or $2 if it was buttered during the California gold rush. Today that same equivalent is worth $28 and $56.

132.   Let's gather here to thank Norway for its good work in the life of a teen. That's an irony! Norway sends out over 5,000 teens annually to a refugee camp simulation for just a day to give them a new perception of life.

133.   Ancient Rome had the best punishment for Parricide (killing a father) called "Poena cullei or penalty of the sack". This is a death penalty where the condemned is sewn in a sack with a cock, and viper and tossed in a river.

134.   Korean legends will say "Back when tigers used to smoke," instead of "Once upon a time."

135.   There are no other species on earth that love to meal prep and cleanup like Americans. The

average American spends a minimum of 37 mins daily doing the above, this is about half the sum of time spent in the 1960s.

136. Ancient Greece, Egypt, and Rome began the practice of pouring some drink on the ground signifying respect for dead friends and relatives known as "Libation." Does the dead drink those drinks?

137. France is the most visited nation with over 89 million annual tourists.

138. In Armenia, children aged 6 and above are taught chess at school, it is a prerequisite part of their curriculum.

139. Thai prisoners are freed early if they take part in special kickboxing matches against foreigners.

140. It's an urban myth that driving a vehicle barefooted is unlawful in the US.

141. The drinking age in Wisconsin is 21.

142. In North Korea, residents are forced to pick one of 28 government-approved haircuts.

143.   The Ethiopian calendar is seven to eight years behind.

144.   Police stations in China use geese in place of guard dogs to keep watch at night.

145.   Filipinos are the world's most prolific gin drinkers.

146.   Mumbai is the only city in the world to have a fully functioning national park.

147.   In Sweden, your car headlights are to be on all the time when driving, even in broad daylight.

148. Did you know that James Bond murdered over 352 people and slept with 52 women? From 007 movies, Dr. No, to Quantum of Solace.

149. You'd wonder why Tom Brady will agree to sell his customized stretch Escalade which stands at $300,000. It has five back seats, and two VIP electric recliners with hand-concealed burl wood folding tables.

150. Snuff films are movies of people being killed, though it was said to have never existed. There stands a one-million-dollar prize money for anyone that can advance with a money-making sold snuff film.

151. The screenwriter for the movie "Cast Away" isolated himself on an island for research, until a volleyball washed up on shore fueled his inspiration for "Wilson."

152. The camera crew of Disney wanted to see the suicidal behavior of lemmings and did a documentary in 1958.

153. Did you know that fake cocaine is more harmful than real coke? A well-known actor, Jonah Hill had to be taken to the hospital for bronchitis

after he sniffed too much fake cocaine at the filming of The Wolf of Wall Street.

154.   Having Alfred Hitchcock on your movie set costs a fortune. He throws his tea cup and saucer away to shatter to the ground after each cup of tea he takes.

155.   Does any actor you know have a cookbook dedicated to him? Well, Brad Pitt has one, this is a collection of all the food he has eaten in the movies he was cast in. His cookbook is called 'Fat Brad the Cookbook.'

156.   Christoph Waltz is his voice actor in the German and French dubs of Inglourious Basterds and Django Unchained.

157.   Charlie Sheen reached an agreement with Warner Bros. and was paid for not doing Two and a Half Men.

158.   Movie popcorn costs more per ounce than filet mignon.

159.   While shooting the Blues Brothers movie, they budgeted for cocaine.

160.   Dwayne Johnson (The Rock) became the selfie king after the premiere of his movie San Andreas.

161. Have you been searching for the most pirated series? Look no further, it's the season 8 premiere of "The Game of Thrones" which was pirated close to 55 million times in just one day.

162. Arnold made $75,000 for his role in Terminator, but in Terminator 2 he made $15,000,000 almost 7 years later.

163. In a 1964 classic – The Navajo extras; John Ford western said stupid and vulgar things on film in serious scenes as no one on set knew their language.

164. Russian Special Services still use typewriters to evade online shadowing.

165. The script writers of the Jurassic Park movie played with our minds, by making us believe that velociraptors were gigantic. In reality, they weren't even bigger than turkeys.

166. One of the first pitched names for Hannah Montana was Alexis Texas.

167. During the 1st season of 'Fresh Prince of Bel-Air,' Will Smith memorized the lines of everyone in the cast.

168.   Unlike the common belief we were forced to take, lemmings do not throw themselves off cliffs.

169.   Animators and visual effects artists for Disney's Frozen were sent to Jackson Hole, Wyoming to practice walking, running, and falling in deep snow.

170.   The initial drawing of Scooby-Doo by Iwao Takamoto made the Great Dane appear as the opposite of what a breeder will desire... having bowed legs, a hump back, and a tiny chin.

171.   Did you know that the disclaimer "No animals were harmed during the making of this film" can be put on movies, even if animals died in the production if cameras weren't rolling at the time?

172.   Netflix is about to launch a DIY project "Netflix and Chill" button called The Switch! When it is activated, the lights dim, your phone is set at do-not-disturb, food is ordered for delivery, and Netflix is set for streaming.

173.   Did you know that the TV series Hannibal has a scene of a naked whipped couple? NBC saw this as inappropriate because their butt cracks showed. So they covered it with blood. As if that was any better!

MOVIES WITH THE GREATEST SOUNDTRACKS

174.   Boogie nights' soundtrack by PT Anderson contains the tonal correspondent of an epiphany. It captures the reminiscence of the late 70s and the corruption of the early 80s.

175.   Spinal Tap's soundtrack was a true legend due to the crazy hilarious focus of their superbly known imitations of almost every genre in music. This was a fun time with a rich parody.

176.   Michael Jackson wrote: "Do The Bartman" after calling the producers of "The Simpsons" but didn't receive credit for it.

177.   Velvet Goldmine's soundtrack is songs mimicking the Thin White Duke. It was a flawless classic mixture of Lou Reed, Iggy Pop, T. Rex, and other contributors who captured the soul of 1970s England.

178.   Samuel L. Jackson was to have an afro in Pulp Fiction but his production assistant didn't know the difference between an afro and a Jheri curl.

179.   All the videos on Netflix are subtitled because the National Association of the Deaf filed a class-action lawsuit against them in 2010.

180.   PG-13 movies can tolerate one "fuck", any more receives an R rating.

181.   The most famous soundtrack is a 70s rock mixtape Led Zeppelin mingles alongside Elton John and Iggy Pop on this masterwork courtesy of Cameron Crowe, who knows a little about rock and roll.

182.   Rushmore's soundtrack is a combination of your nostalgic picks like the Who and the Kinks plus a dash of Mark Mothersbough.

183.   Neil deGrasse Tyson condemned the scene in "Titanic" where Rose looks at the night sky after the ship sank; saying the position of the stars wasn't accurate.

184.   SpongeBob SquarePant's character Squidward Tentacles has six tentacles, making him neither squid nor octopus.

185.   In the film 'Thank You for Smoking', none of the acts are ever seen smoking.

186.   American beauty's soundtrack had a strong message that keeps you glued to the movie. Bob Dylan began and then the choral Beatles ended the amazing score.

187.   Barry Lyndon's score won an Oscar for Best Adapted Score. It is the best addition to contemporary romanticism that leaves its listeners captivated even after a long.

188.   The US Witness Protection Program hasn't breached security in which a protected person or family member was harmed.

189.   The Big Lebowski's soundtrack is a crazy mixture of tunes that is never outdated. The Coens show their admiration for the Rolling Stones and their fake hatred for country rock in this great ode to the bright side of darkness.

190.   The greatest soundtrack of the 60s is America Graffiti ... From soul to blues and rock.

191.   Vin Diesel showed Steven Spielberg a video of his self-directed short movie with a letter about his respect for the director.

192.   2001: A Space Odyssey is a beautiful soundtrack best heard while the movie is being viewed. This is a feast of intellectual waltzes and huge classics that rises in romanticism with each passing year.

193.   A break from the greatest soundtracks... Alex Trebek the host of Jeopardy holds the world record for the most game show episodes hosted by him

and never takes sick leave for the 34 years of his 6,800 episodes.

194.   The hit TV show — Stranger Things was discarded 15 to 20 times by many networks before Netflix finally gave them a chance.

195.   Did you know that Gentil Garçon the French artist worked with a paleontologist, named François Escuilié for Pac-Man? They created a skull of the pellet-gobbling video game icon, Pac-Man. Now we know!

196.   Ages ago, Hulk Hogan missed a call from his agent to promote a new indoor grill who then gave it to George Foreman.

197.   Annually, Walt Disney World's Lost and Found gathers more than 3,500 digital cameras, 6,000 cell phones, and 18,000 hats. That's a lot of lost items if you ask me!

198.   There was a batman villain named Condiment King, he was defeated by slipping on his ketchup.

199.   Pixar credits its achievement to its anti-Disney method of no songs, no happy village, and no love story.

200. In 2015, Dwayne Johnson (The Rock) broke the world record for the most selfies taken in three minutes with 105 snaps. Now the record stands at 168.

201. Toy Story 3's Lots-o'-Huggin bear was formerly meant to appear in the first film, but the equipment needed to animate his fur did not yet exist.

202. Ben Affleck left college after his creative writing teacher mocked an early draft of the Good Will Hunting screenplay.

203. Michael Jackson offered to write Bart a number-one single.

204. Christian Bale refused the role of James Bond, saying "I've already played a serial killer."

205. The actors that played Mickey and Minnie Mouse were married in the real world.

206. MTV's 16 and pregnant has been related to a drop in teen pregnancies.

207. Actor John Cusack trained in kickboxing for above 20 years and is a sixth-degree black belt.

FACTS ABOUT THE NOTORIOUS CRIME WORLD

208.	Ever heard of the notorious "Highway Killer"? Its Larry Eyler, he killed twenty-one men so far. He'd lure men into his car and have them beaten and gutted. He was sentenced to die by lethal injection but died of AIDS.

209.	John Willis is chilling in federal prison for drug trafficking after being introduced to Ping On, Boston's Chinese mafia by a young Asian. He's now called "White Devil" and knows Chinese.

210.	Why would anyone have to go to jail for food? Well, a Texas man got 50 years for stealing $1.2 million worth of fajitas.

211.	Meet the Yorkshire Ripper named Peter Sutcliffe who began his killing career in 1975. Forgive me, but the satire was intended. He molested and killed his victims with ball-peen hammers, knives, and screwdrivers.

212.	Let's welcome the Japanese criminal ninja who robbed 254 homes and stole goods worth $260,000. Unfortunately, this 74-year-old ninja was caught by the feds.

213.   Oscar Romero was an archbishop in the El Salvador Catholic Church where he upheld human rights and was against injustice in the U.S. He was assassinated during mass to send a message to his supporters.

214.   A long time ago in Egypt, during the rule of Ptolemy II, books from the ships are confiscated and a copy is made. Then the copied version is sent to the owner, while the original copies are kept in the library of Alexandria.

215.   The acclaimed killer clown is John Wayne Gacy. He spent most of his life in jail. He had Rick Staton as his special art dealer, becoming one of the first of America's top collectors of murderabilia.

216.   No jokes, criminals can turn out to be the best behaved. The Australian initial police force called the Night Watch comprised 12 of the best-behaved criminals.

217.   Olof Palme was an outspoken advocate of passionate regulation and investigation of Sweden's nuclear energy program and Sweden's prime minister from 1982-1986. He was killed and his killer was never caught.

218.   A pod of orcas in SE Australia killed Eden. They often assisted local whales to kill baleen whales from 1840 and 1930. The whalers left the

carcass for the orcas to feed on the lips and tongues known as the "law of the tongue".

219.   Archduke Ferdinand attempted to assassinate people and failed, the bomb leaped off the car and blew up under the wrong car. Ferdinand ran for safety to a riverbed and threw up his suicide pill.

220.   Marcus Julius Brutus connived with other senators to murder Gaius Julius Caesar in Rome. He was stabbed by over sixty men on March 15, 44 BC called the "Ides of March."

221.   Horn shark in a baby stroller, what a sight! Sometimes in San Antonio, thieves stole a little horn shark from an Aquarium and smuggled it put with a baby stroller.

222.   Serial killer Ed Kemper made friends with the police officers investigating his murders. They called him "Big Ed."

223.   Two students were arrested for a plan to poison Chicago's water supply with typhoid, anthrax, and various other pathogens in 1972.

224.   Gerald Schaefer was a policeman who sexually assaulted and killed over thirty women.

225.   Meet the Vietnam War sniper named Carlos Hathcock but popularly called "White Feather." He crawled for 3 days to kill a general across 2000m.

226.   The popular Genesee River Killer whose real name is Arthur Shawcross began to kill without control while fighting during the Vietnam War. He killed and ate two Vietnamese girls, and killed many prostitutes too.

227.   Three al-Qaeda gunmen shot Mike Day a Navy SEAL officer 27 times and were made unconscious by a grenade. When he became conscious he killed two of them and escaped. Today he is doing well.

228.   Back in 1957, Philadelphians in Susquehanna experienced great shock at the sight of the brutally mutilated 6-year-old white boy found dead in a cardboard box. The case stands unsolved to date.

229.   Wouldn't you want to join a soccer team that offers winning prizes such as soaps, sugar, and goats? Well, a Ugandan prison has a soccer league with 10 formal teams and a body (UPSA).

230.   This Scottish serial killer named Dennis Nilsen invites men to his house, has sexual activity with them, and kills them out of fear of being alone the next day.

231. A New York City man was released, after being held in jail for transporting child pornography, when porn star Lupe Fuentes flew from Spain to show up at his trial with her ID and passport to prove her age.

232. Following the fall of Nanking and China, the Rape of Nanking took place for over six weeks with the Japanese Army. Looting, rape, arson, and public execution caused the death of over 250,000 people.

233. Bobby Joe Long and his mother had carnal knowledge of each other when he was thirteen years old. After then he began to target married women, raped fifty of them, and killed nine. He got a death sentence.

234. Shorty the temporary Cross Dresser! Shorty was a drug trafficker who was caught disguised as a teenage girl trying to escape a Rio de Janeiro prison.

235. Carl Panzram is one of America's most violent and vicious serial killers who regretted not being dead or born at all.

236. Meet Aitzaz Hassan who saved 2000 of his schoolmates from a suicide bomber. This 15-year-old Pakistani schoolboy stopped the bomber by the school gate.

237.   When notorious murderer Carl Panzram was condemned to death, he didn't appeal and threatened to kill any activists who tried to intervene for him.

238.   Fritz Haarmann took advantage of a runaway named Friedel Roth. Fritz sexually assaulted her, chopped her head off, and placed it by the stove. Five years later, he confessed.

239.   The St. Bartholomew's Day massacre On August 24, 1572, lasted for many months and resulted in the death of over 5000 people.

240.   John Robinson, a sadomasochist deceives women from the internet and sexually assaults them. Two containers were found in his Kansas home containing bodies of females.

241.   The famed Vampire of Dusseldorf's real name is Peter Kurten. Peter killed over thirty women after sexually assaulting them. He died by the guillotine.

MEDICAL PROCEDURES & ABNORMALITIES

242. Did you know there's an uncommon disorder that duplicates the face on the head? It's called Diprospus and is caused by a protein called sonic hedgehog homolog. What a name!

243. It's a good thing to know that a new alternative cancer therapy is being researched. It consists of injecting dead cells into the body to help the immune cells target cancer.

244. Fetus in fetu is a rare abnormality where a twin gets conjoined (internally or partly externally) to its twin while inside the mother's womb. There's a popular case in India by Sanju Bhagat.

245. Are you a rich man? Then you must love small breasts. Well, 2013 research has it that poor men love big breasts while rich men love smaller breasts.

246. When a part of the vagina is medically taken out due to cancer or for sexual reassignment surgeries; that process is called Vaginectomy.

247. Have you been forgetting the names of the most common thing lately? Then you may need to

check with the doctor if you have a medical condition called Anomia.

248. Some men are allergic to their semen and they showcase flu-like symptoms after each ejaculation.

249. There is a rare chronic sleep disorder called Fatal Familial Insomnia, which renders the victim unable to sleep.

250. The most popular case of proteus syndrome is that of Joseph Merrick often called the Elephant Man. This condition makes the skin and bone grow excessively, often causing tumors.

251. Agnosia is a misidentification principle discovered by Oxford University experts that says when we are blindfolded, it's hard to spot the toe that is poked.

252. When a part of the penis is medically taken out due to cancer or to correct a botched circumcision, that process is called Penectomy.

253. When the facial muscles get paralyzed is called Möbius syndrome. This is an uncommon disorder that keeps its sufferers from having any facial expressions.

254.   The strongest muscle in the body is the tongue.

255.   Some migraines have no pain they are called silent migraines.

256.   Caffeine is a painkiller, and when used with other painkillers, like Acetaminophen or NSAIDs, potentiates their effects significantly.

257.   Smallpox is the first and only disease that has ever been eradicated.

258.   Research has it that fat king penguins are more unsteady on their feet.

259.   Have you seen children looking like old men/women? It's Hutchinson-Gilford progeria syndrome (progeria), and it is a disorder that triggers premature aging.

260.   Initially, Opium was meant to be a non-addictive drug to manage people with addiction come out of it.

261.   Did you know that Viagra was formerly created to treat a heart disease called Angina? This was by raising the blood circulation to the heart, but it wasn't successful.

262.   Some Robots gave Professor Jacques Marescaux and his team from the IRCAD a helping hand on the 7th of Sept 2001 in France to carry out a gallbladder surgery. This was the first of its kind called The Lindbergh Operation.

263.   Cutaneous porphyria is a condition that causes excess hair, blisters, inflammation, and rotting of the skin. It can cause red-colored teeth and fingernails, and after exposure to the sun, urine can turn purple, pink, brown, or black.

264.   Ever heard of people who have sexual relationships with corpses? They are Necrophilia. The odd sexual attraction to corpses is called Necrophilia.

265.   It is spelled "Elephantiasis" and not elephant-itis! This is a very common disability that is showcased by the thickening of the skin and it is caused by parasitic worms passed from mosquito bites.

266.   The US has approximately 100,000 patients awaiting a kidney transplant and up till now over 2,000 kidneys are thrown away every year, the reasons being that about 1/5th of the recipient are nowhere to be found.

267.   Fibrodysplasia ossificans progressiva has no cure. It is a very uncommon disease that makes

parts of the body such as the ligaments, and muscles become bone when they go bad.

268.   Dynamically, the amniotic fluid in the womb of a mother can be nearly a liter of fluids at 30+ weeks and gets replaced every 3 hours close to the end of pregnancy.

269.   Dr. Barry J. Marshall drank the Helicobacter pylori bacterium to prove to the medical community that ulcers weren't caused by stomach acid.

270.   Medical disorders and their lengthy names! Wow! Lewandowsky-Lutz dysplasia (also known as epidermodysplasia verruciformis) is an extremely rare inheritable disorder in which multitudes of warts forms on the skin.

271.   Here is a very rare condition where a male is born with two penises called Diphallia.

272.   If you sneeze very hard, you can break a rib. If you try to subdue a sneeze, you can rupture a blood vessel in your head or neck and die.

273.   Dr. Werner a Brazilian doctor used 3d printing to aid blind parents to feel their baby's ultrasound using GE ultrasound machines.

274.   Did you know that one in four people has a hole in their heart? This disorder is called Patent Foramen Ovale (PFO), which has been there since they were newborns.

275.   Adermatoglyphia, also known as immigration delay disease allows its victims to be birthed without fingerprints.

276.   The spinning will just remind me of the story of Snow-white. The spinning wheel is believed to have its roots in India from the 13th century.

277.   Don't you just want to be a British monarch you get to celebrate their birthdays twice a year? One is celebrated on their birth date & then an official parade in his honor.

278.   King Tut is the only mummy from ancient Egypt that was mummified with a decent erection. What a sight that would be!

279.   There was an all-black troop in WWI that the Germans dreaded so much and called the "Harlem Hellfighters".

280.   Mississippi only endorsed the 13th amendment, which ended slavery back in 1865, and 1995. But, they never officially informed the US Archivist and so it had to be rectified and was finally approved in 2013.

281.   History has it that there are more slaves today than were ever on the surface of this earth. Slavery meant there are unfree laborers whose services cost around ninety dollars.

282.   The "Sean's Bar" is a bar in Ireland that opened in the year 900 A.D. and is still operational.

283.   It was never expected by the Navy that the oceanographer will discover the Titanic. Titanic's wreck was discovered during the Cold War.

284.   The first quarantine happened in the 14th century in Venice. This was to stop the advancement of a plague.

285.   A 102-year-old German woman is the oldest to bag a Ph.D. She was prohibited from attending her final oral exam in 1938 by the Nazi-influenced university because she was Jewish.

286.   After the fall of Berlin in WW2, there were a lot of rape cases that led to the birth of over 100,000 children.

287.   12% of Québec is freshwater, which is 3% of all of the world's freshwater.

288.   Saudi Arabia erected a special "Anti-Witchcraft Unit" and a telephone hotline for the public to report mystical evils.

289.   The movable type and paper were first used by the Chinese.

290.   The Science Guy - Bill Nye only has a Bachelor's degree in Science but has been awarded three honorary doctorate degrees.

291.   The meaning of 18th-century word – leint means to "urinate in an alcoholic beverage to grow its power".

292.   Thomas Crapper isn't the inventor of toilets like many people think. Crapper was a plumber, but Alexander Cummings takes the credit as the inventor of this illustrious gadget.

293.   In 2005, the cardboard box was welcomed into the "National Toy Hall of Fame".

294.   Oxford University is older than the Aztec civilization. Founded in 1249

295.   The first female congressman was the only person who voted against going to war with Japan and also voted against WWI.

296.   On Sept 27, 1986, almost 1.5 million balloons were released into the air in Cleveland to break the Guinness Book of Records.

297.   The U.S. and Canada fought the bloodless "war of pork and beans" in 1839.

298.   On April fool's Day, 1976, the BBC persuaded many listeners that a special placement of the planets would briefly reduce gravity on Earth.

299.   For 90 years, El Azizia in northern Libya held the record for the hottest place on Earth.

300.   Ireland's population still hasn't returned to what it was before the Potato Famine.

301.   The Algerian national anthem was initially written in blood on a prison cell wall by an Algerian revolutionary that was imprisoned by the French colonial regime.

302.   In a deck of playing cards, each king represents a great king from history.

303.   NASA re-labeled the penis sleeve for urinating in space suits from "small, medium, and large" to "large, gigantic, and humongous" because astronauts only picked the large and they kept slipping off.

304.   Research has it that a clam projected to be 507 years old, the oldest-ever living animal, and mistakenly killed it.

305.   In the 1950s, Canada abruptly canceled the development of its fighter jet (Avro Arrow) in favor of nuclear missiles (Bomarcs).

306.   There is a 372 pages lengthy "proof" that 1+1=2 is 372.

307.   The extreme rationing in England in WWII reduced infant mortality by ensuring nutrition for everyone.

308.   A city in Texas changed its name to "DISH, Texas" to receive free Dish Satellite service for 10 years.

309.   The first woman to win two Nobel Prize awards was Marie Curie and still wasn't legally allowed to go to college as a woman, so she went to the secret Polish Flying University.

310.   In 1968, Kim IL Sung sent 31 commandos to South Korea to try and assassinate the president.

311.   Who is the most famous notorious murderer in history? I'd say it's *Jack the Ripper* who was never caught.

312.   Costa Rica eliminated its military and conveyed the military budget toward education, healthcare, and environmental protection over 65 years ago.

313.   A national survey carried out in the 1990s found that Mario was more recognizable to American children than Mickey Mouse.

314.   When pirates used the red flag, it means "no quarter given", or no mercy would be shown and no life would be spared.

315.   There's a small sculpture on the moon named "Fallen Astronaut" made by Belgian artist Paul Van Hoeydonck and put by the crew of Apollo 15 in 1971.

316.   There is a city in Kansas called Gas. Their approved motto is "Don't Pass Gas, Stop and Enjoy It".

317.   Over seventy-five million people globally died at the hands of a deadly pandemic called the Bubonic Plague but popularly called The Black Death.

318.   Did you know Edgar Allen Poe sold his poem The Raven for $9 to The American Review, before that, the owner of Graham's Magazine gifted him $15 for refusing Poe because he felt the poem was a cry for help?

319.   The first British spy notorious as 007 was Dr. John Dee, in 1560. Queen Elizabeth called him "my eyes".

320.   On 5 April 2010, four women were in space at the same time. This was the biggest female meeting off the planet.

321.   The richest man in history was Musa I (1312 – 1337) of Mali in Africa.

322.   Antikythera Mechanism is the earliest common example of a mechanical calculator used to calculate astronomical objects.

323.   One time in 1936 there was a book that weighed ~2 1/2 tons. It was called the Golden Book of Cleveland, it had 6,000 pages, was 3 feet thick and it was 7 feet by 5 feet.

324.   Genghis Khan's chief adviser was a seized scholar named Yelu Chucai.

325.   Mercy dogs also known as casualty dogs were trained and used during WW1. The dogs tended to the injured by taking medical supplies to them or staying with the wounded.

326.   Hans Redl, a tennis player with one arm played at Wimbledon from 1947 to 1956. He was able to play by throwing the ball up with his racket.

327.   Juan Pujol García was a rogue spy during WWII. Britain's MI5 turned down his offer to be

their spy and he went and spied on Germany however as a double agent.

328.   Historically, Mother's Day is the busiest day for regular phone calls, while Father's Day is the busiest day for collecting calls.

329.   The official firehouse dog is Dalmatian because in the 18th century they would run along with horse-drawn "fire engines" and stop other dogs or animals from scaring the horses.

330.   In 1980 during the Mount St. Helens eruption, photographer Robert Landsberg knew he couldn't survive, so he laid above his equipment to save the photographs he had taken earlier of the happenings.

331.   The Great Dome (Volkshalle) is the People's hall, it was a colossal monumental building designed by Adolf Hitler and Albert Speer his architect for Berlin, Germany. The war came and the Great Dome was never built.

332.   The world's largest snowflake was 15 inches in diameter and 8 inches thick seen in Fort Keogh, Montana in 1887. It made it into the Guinness Book of Records.

333.   The notion that breakfast is the most important meal of the day arose from General

Foods' attempt to sell more nuts, grapes, and cereal during its 1944 marketing campaign.

334.   Initially, the first set of knives was created from flaking rocks. None of them made it.

335.   The White House used to be partly driven by solar panels early in 1979.

336.   On April 1, 2007, Google circulated an email to its employees cautioning that a python was loose in its New York Office.

337.   8th January 1836 is the last day in history that the USA had no national debt.

338.   The Germans conquered Denmark very quickly in 1940, the Danes had no time to officially declare war against them and surrendered in 2 hours.

339.   The first and the last British soldiers to die in WWI are unexpectedly buried only 15 feet apart.

340.   The Lakota People have tried to claim independence in the longest legal battle in history (more than 160 years) with the United States.

341.   The world's biggest diamond was conveyed from Africa to England by sea and was broadcasted as a rouse. The real diamond was posted by mail.

342.   The oldest set of stone tools was found by Archeologists who called them olduwan. This dates far back 1.5 million BC.

343.   In 1871, Mr. Ramon Artagaveytia endured the fire and sinking of a ship that left him emotionally scarred.

344.   If you die homeless or poor in New York City, you are buried by prisoners on Hart Island in a mass grave.

345.   The USSR victoriously sent a spacecraft and entry probe to Venus in 1966 making it the first space probe to hit the surface of another planet - three years before the US put a man on the moon.

346.   US ZIP Code 12345 belongs to the main corporate campus of General Electric.

347.   The term "noon" is gotten from the Latin nona hora or ninth hour.

348.   Hawaii tried to pass a law keeping the legal smoking age to 100 in early 2019.

349.   What would you do if you had all your dog's poop gathered and mailed a lost property box for not picking after them when you take them for a

walk? That's what the town of Brunete near Madrid does.

350.   There is a museum in Massachusetts that exhibits bad art that is "too bad to be ignored"

351.   The name of America's #1 WWII Flying Ace was Dick Bong.

352.   Volkswagen has manufactured currywurst at its Wolfsburg plant since 1973. The sausage is branded as a "Volkswagen Original Part' with its part number.

353.   A Romanian Engineer designed his first flying machine in 1902 Traian Vuia and then presented his plan to the Académie des Sciences in Paris in 1903.

354.   The USA bombed China's embassy in Belgrade, killing three Chinese journalists in 1999.

355.   Lizzie's father was axed eleven times and her stepmother eighteen times but Lizzie didn't do it unlike popular opinion has it. Another murder took place while in custody, so she was set free.

356.   Zambia had a space program in the 1960s made up of a grade school science teacher, a teenage girl and her cat, and a missionary.

357.   This is a weird business strategy but it worked! DMA Design/Rockstar Games released Grand Theft Auto, and they paid reviewers to publish negative reviews about the game to keep it controversial and popular.

358.   The most radioactive places at Chernobyl are still the hospital rooms where the clothes of the responders and equipment used to clean the debris from the explosion lay.

359.   In 2017 during the North American eclipse, researchers discovered that just moments before totality, all the bees stopped buzzing till it passed.

360.   The shortest war on record was fought between Zanzibar and England in 1896. Zanzibar surrendered after 38 minutes and about 500 casualties.

361.   The Indus Valley Civilization was a developed culture that lived peaceably with the great civilizations of Mesopotamia.

362.   In 2006, Honda became the sole supplier of engines in the IndyCar series.

363.   The "Fallen Astronaut" is the only sculpture on the moon, yet it remains pretty anonymous.

364.   There is proof that early humans were killed and eaten by eagles.

365.   In Welsh, the word for the week is wythnos, which means "eight nights". Historically, the week started and ended with night.

366.   The last duel in Canada was between two men in 1837. After one shot the other, he fainted. The guns were loaded with blanks.

367.   Icelanders can effortlessly read Old Norse, a dead language spoken in Scandinavia over 1000 years ago.

368.   Oktoberfest happened as a wedding reception for a Prince in Bavaria in 1810, and from then it became a yearly event.

369.   Arnold Schwarzenegger wasn't permitted to dub his role in Terminator to German as he was seen as a backwoodsman.

370.   Aeschylus is the foremost of the three ancient Greek playwrights whose work is still used today.

371.   In 1955, Federal agents arrested John Gilbert Graham for blowing up an airplane but found out that it wasn't a federal crime to blow up an airplane.

372.   General Electric (GE) accepts thousands of Santa letters each year from kids trusting it would make the most sense for Santa's workshop to have 12345 as his ZIP code.

373.   The Bubonic Plague was caused by the bacterium Yersinia pestis from 1347-1351.

374.   During WW2, captured German officers who were sent to Britain as POWs lived in luxury in Trent Park.

375.   Fire is the most important discovery of man since 1,000,000 BC ago.

376.   Pavarotti holds the record for curtain calls doing 165 after a performance of the Donizetti opera "L'elisir d'amore" at the Deutsche Oper Berlin in 1988.

377.   The oldest unbroken alliance in the world is between England and Portugal dating back to 1373.

378.   American Airlines saved $40,000 in 1987 by removing one olive from every salad served in first class.

379.   The Huns had no writing organism, thus all records of them were written by their enemies who

universally described them as nearly monstrous in every way.

380.   37 years before Pearl Harbor, Japan launched a surprise attack on Russia, destroying many of the Russian fleets at Port Arthur.

381.   Snoopy used the phrase 'Cowabunga!' in the 1950s before the Teenage Mutant Ninja Turtles used it as their slogan in the 1980s.

382.   With a fee of $25 Hawaii allows people to throw their beloved's ashes into their volcanoes, but it has to be done discreetly.

383.   Napoleon Bonaparte's penis was detached from his corpse during the autopsy, displayed at a museum, and finally sold for $2,700 in the 1970s.

384.   University of Melbourne Archaeologists have discovered 15 new sites in Laos holding more than a hundred 1000-year-old massive stone jars possibly used to "bury" the dead.

385.   A US Elite soldier climbed 95-foot cliffs below Point Du Hoc to seize and destroy key German strongholds in the D-Day assault on June 6, 1944.

386.   When General Sheridan said, "The only good Indian is a dead Indian." What he meant is alleged, "The only good Indians I ever saw were dead."

387.   Rolling Stone magazine originally gave Nirvana's Nevermind a 3-star rating in 1991. They now give it 5 stars and rank it as the 17th greatest album of all time.

388.   The Pillars of Creation, a nebula 7,000 light years away, was wrecked by a supernova 6,000 years ago.

389.   Quentin Tarantino's '64 Chevy Malibu was stolen from the set of Pulp Fiction in 1994.

390.   Paul Geidel charged with second-degree murder was first incarcerated at age 17 and finally released at age 86.

391.   Indus Valley Civilization moved from Western India to Afghanistan.

392.   North Korea has only 8 internet hosts while Vatican City has 107. The USA has the most out of any country with over 500 million.

393.   After 13 years of attempting to find the framework of a protein, scientists created an online competitive game called Foldit that asked gamers to try and solve it. The framework was then found in 3 weeks.

394. British astronomer and chemist, Warren de la Rue, enclosed a platinum coil in a vacuum tube and passed an electric current through it in 1840, thus creating the world's first lightbulb...forty years before Edison.

395. Thunder-plump is an early 19th-century Scottish word meaning a heavy and sudden shower of rain followed by thunder and lightning.

396. There is a clock being built on a mountain that is designed to tick for 10,000 years and play a unique melody that is never repeated.

397. Each Rolls-Royce pinstripe is painted by Englishman Mark Court, a former village sign painter.

398. In 1990, Dr. Dre attacked a woman over an interview using Ice Cube.

399. The Crooked Forest is located in Poland and is home to hundreds of pine trees planted in the 1930s which are mysteriously curved at a 90° angle.

400. There are only six long-term skywriters, those who use aircraft to expel special smoke during a flight in patterns that create visible words from the ground, left in the world.

401.   11% of the World's gold is held by Indian housewives. This is more than the reserves of IMF, Switzerland, the USA, and Germany put together.

402.   In the 1920s, Hugo Gernsback invented The Isolator which was a helmet aimed to improve concentration by blocking out noise and narrowing the user's field of view.

403.   Study shows that 48% of Thailand's Buddhist monks are overweight.

404.   There has only one successful shoot-down of an F-117A stealth plane, in 1999 during the NATO bombing of past Yugoslavia.

405.   Hotel La Montaña Mágica is a unique hotel built to mimic a volcano and even erupt water.

406.   Scientists that studied the ocean floor in the Black Sea have discovered over 40 ships, some from as far back as the 9th century.

407.   Instant ramen was created in Japan in 1958 by Momofuku Ando.

408.   The Ethiopian calendar is 7 years behind the Gregorian calendar due to them having the 13th month of either 5 or 6 days (in the case of a leap year). The new millennium was celebrated on Sept. 12, 2007.

409.   During the ninth century, the hourglass was one of the first portable and reusable methods of determining time.

410.   Tulsa, Oklahoma once had a "Black Wall Street" that was formerly the most economically prosperous black community in America.

411.   Nike put a clause in Michael Jordan's rookie contract: "be rookie of the year, average 20 points per game, be an all-star, or sell $4 mill worth of shoes in a year."

412.   In 1980, a volcanologist died at an observation camp when Mount St. Helens exploded.

413.   In the Vietnam War, a US task force known as 'Tiger Force' usually cut off the ears of its victims to make necklaces from them.

414.   Nazi soldiers burned civilians alive in the town of Oradour-Sur-Glane in WW2.

415.   In 2013, Disney abandoned its policy of letting disabled people skip lines in its theme parks, after rampant abuse of the rule by people hiring disabled "tour guides" to skip waiting in lines for rides.

416. The true 'friendship tree' between US President Trump and French President Macron died in quarantine once uprooted after the ceremonial planting. But Macron is sending a replacement oak tree.

417. Stewardesses is the lengthiest word typed with just the left hand.

418. A '64 Chevy Malibu was recovered in 2013.

419. Lyndon Johnson was the first President sworn in by a woman and it happened on Air Force One after Kennedy's assassination.

420. The term "plastic surgery" was coined in 1839, 70 years before plastic was even invented.

421. Alphabet Inc.'s web address is abc.xyz and they are Google's parent company.

422. The term "soccer" was initially used in England before the Americans adopted it.

423. More than 960 bamboo slips from the Han Dynasty (206 BC-AD 25) were found with more than 25,000 characters detailing basic theories of traditional Chinese medicine, acupuncture, and prescription, as well as a book on law.

424.   The mummified body of bank robber Elmer McCurdy was found in an amusement park by a TV crew in 1975. It had been mistaken for a wax mannequin. Elmer died in 1911.

425.   Bulletproof vests, windshield wipers, fire escapes, and laser printers were all invented by women.

426.   Millennials between the ages of 18-34 are more likely to live with their parents instead of a spouse/partner. This is the first time this has been true of this age demographic since record-keeping began in the 1880s.

427.   According to the CIA's 2013 data, the United States has 13,513 airports (recognizable from the air), which is more than the next 10 countries combined.

428.   Once ketchup is branded "Fancy" it's truly a United States Department of Agriculture grade connoting it's thicker than standard ketchup.

429.   Today, Jordan scored 28.2 points per game, was named all-star, and Nike sold $100 mill of shoes in 1984-85.

430.   The longest-serving prisoner in American history was Paul Geidel, who served 68 years and

245 days between 1911 and 1980 for second-degree murder.

431.   Mount Kosciuszko remains the highest mountain in Australia.

432.   The U.S. does not use bills above $100 since President Nixon made it difficult to move huge amounts of money through borders for drug trading.

433.   In World War 2, a Luftwaffe pilot refused to destroy a spoilt B-17.

434.   The NHL made a puck with IR sensors in it to track it and made it glow.

435.   In WW2, German field marshal, Erwin Rommel often pilots himself in a reconnaissance aircraft over the battle to assess the situation.

436.   At the end of World War 2, the Japanese started to use pine oil from pine tree roots to fuel their airplanes.

437.   Take out all the boxes currently in the cabinet and vacuum them to get rid of dry food spills and cobwebs.

438.   Mix 2 tablespoons dish of liquid with half a cup of water and use a sponge to dip and wipe inside the cabinet. Follow it up with a dry sponge rub.

439.   To get rid of the pasty muck that can gather on the cabinet doors, mix 2 tablespoons of baking soda with 10 drops of mineral oil. Then go in with a toothbrush to dip in it and scrub.

440.   To get rid of the damp smells that often gather inside the cabinet, mix 2 parts of vodka with 3 parts of vinegar. Go in with your sponge dip and wipe. Continue with a dry sponge wipe.

441.   To protect your cabinets from spills, put cling film under the boxes or aluminum foil, to help attract the spills.

442.   To have a tidy kitchen sink, clean your steel/porcelain sinks by sprinkling sea salt and adding some squeezed lemon juice over it. Let it

stay overnight, in the morning, scrub it with lemon peels and wash it off with warm water.

443. Clean your dirty sink with a mixture of 2 parts hydrogen peroxide (35%) and one part of baking soda. Go in with a toothbrush to dip and scrub.

444. To get rid of scratch marks, dip a cotton gauze in mineral oil and rub over the scrubs. They will vanish without a trace. If the marks are large, then add a little white toothpaste.

445. To free a sink, drop some Alka Seltzer or Pepto Bismol tablets in it. The sink unclog and leave behind a lovely fragrance.

446. To get rid of the sticky stain that forms above the tiles, dip a sponge in mineral oil and wipe over the tiles. You can also apply steel wool in oil and scrub.

447. Another option for the above method is to put butter paper above the tile and place a hot iron over it. The heat from the iron will melt the butter with the dirt and they will both stick to the paper.

448. Or better still, use sandpaper to carefully scrub away the dirt, or use a pumice stone, whichever suits you.

449.   To avoid scuffs on the tiles, make a paste of baking soda and toothpaste, then go in with a little cotton wool and wipe off the scuffs.

450.   When all the stain is out, go in with a sponge in a mixture made of 2 parts of hydrogen peroxide and 3 parts of water to help bleach the tiles.

451.   Make a mixture of baking soda and vinegar to be applied over the countertop of your kitchen. Let it stay for about 30 mins, then wipe it off with a wet sponge.

452.   To clean out your grill and stove, spread some baking soda on it and go in with a sponge in vinegar to wipe. This process takes out the burnt stain and the foul smell.

453.   Clean the inside of your oven by spraying some sea salt at the bottom and drop 2 Pepto Bismol tablets in a cup of water. Pour the mixture over the salt and leave overnight. The next morning, go in with a dry sponge to scrub.

454.   To clean your silverware, put 2 tablespoons of wood ash in a bowl and add in some drops of lemon. Go in with this mix using a toothbrush and scrub the silverware.

455.   To keep the fridge smelling fresh, put a small bowl of baking soda in both the fridge and the

freezer section. You can also put dryer sheets under the shelves to help keep the fridge clean.

456.   Keep your toaster clean by dusting the outsides with the use of a pastry brush and then make a mixture of 2 parts cream of tartar and 2 parts 1 part water and make use of it to clean the exterior of the toaster.

457.   Clean your dishwasher by emptying a little pack of Tang or Kool-Aid and let the washer run for a cycle.

458.   Another alternative to the above is to fill up two little bowls with vinegar and a drop(s) of lemon or orange peels inside. Put one over the top shelf and one below and run the machine for a cycle.

459.   Clean your blender jar, drop in 2 tablespoons of liquid dish wash with a little water, and whizz for a second.

460.   Clean inside your oven by lacing wet tissues inside and running it for a couple of minutes.

461.   Use peanut butter to remove gum from any surface, be it your hair, on the carpet, the sofa, etc.

462.   To eliminate that unpleasant fishy smell from your home, place a tablespoon of peanut butter after frying the fish, drop it in the frying pan, and

fry off for a minute or two. The smell of peanut butter will fill the house.

463.　　An excellent organizing hack to use in your kitchen is using a cutting board as a cover for your dustbin.

464.　　Drill a hole over the counter and put the dustbin under it. Then conceal the hole with a cutting board, this way you can slide the board and all the cuttings will go in the hole.

465.　　To store all your snacks, make use of shoe and jeweler holders.

466.　　Did you know you can microwave your kitchen towels to have those dry much faster and further kill germs inherent?

467.　　To get all the dirt and dry dust from the crannies of your couch, cover a little twig with twin sides tape and use it to run through the length of the couch. All the dust and dirt will stick to it.

468.　　To eliminate the stains from pale-looking sofas, make use of a mixture of baking soda and vinegar and wipe it away.

469.　　You can also use a mixture of hydrogen peroxide with water to clean a white couch.

470.   Use solid sandpaper to pumice stone to take out stains from leather couches. To take out little stains, use a nail file.

471.   For homemade fresheners for your couch, make a mixture of equal parts rose and lavender essential oil and put in some drops of lukewarm water. Go in with the mixture and a sponge to wipe the couch.

472.   To eliminate food stains from your couch, make use of equal parts vinegar and dish liquid and make use of a sponge to wipe off and the stain will leave.

473.   To eliminate oil stains from your couch, sprinkle a little talcum powder above it and use a mixture of vinegar and dish liquid. Use your sponge to wipe it off.

474.   To have a clean floor, make a mixture of half a cup of vinegar and half a cup of hydrogen peroxide/lemon juice and put it in a container. Add warm water to the mixture and go in with a mop to wipe the floor.

475.   Did you know that tough floor stains can be eliminated using a mix of nail polish remover and water? Make this mix and pour it over the stain, leave for an hour and wipe off with a wet cloth or sponge.

476.   Eliminate oil stains from granite/marble floors, and make a paste using vinegar and baking. Apply the mix over the stain, leave it for 30 mins till an hour and wipe off with a wet sponge.

477.   To make your floor shine, make a mix of baby oil and baby shampoo to water, and go in with a mop to wipe the floor.

478.   Add 2 cups of alcohol to a bucket of 5 cups of water and go in with your mop, wipe properly to disinfect your home.

479.   To eliminate dust and dirt from our carpets, use a pet comb by running it against the grain of the carpet.

480.   You can make use of a window scraper to bring out a lot of dirt from the carpet.

481.   For more effective results, you can wrap both sides around a stick and use it to wipe the dust from the carpet.

482.   Sprinkle some powder or flour over food spills or vomit, and leave it to congeal. Go in with a vacuum cleaner, then take a sponge in using a mix of liquid wash and vodka to disinfect and take off foul odor from the carpet.

483. Disinfect your carpets by putting at least 10 drops of eucalyptus oil, 2 tablespoons of water and 5 drops of clove oil into a small spray can then spray over the carpet. Ticks, mosquitoes, and fleas will be at bay!

484. Clean out your fan using an old pillow case over the blade and pull it outwards to collect the dust.

485. Clean out your air conditioner using pressure cans to blow out the dust and dirt.

486. Use some mineral, baby, or roil on a helium balloon and let it float to the ceiling to take out the cobwebs and dust. It will stick to the balloon.

487. Eliminate dirt and dust on window grills, use the blow function in the vacuum cleaner to blow it off.

488. To get rid of blemishes from wallpapers, use a little piece of newly baked bagel and rub it over the paper.

489. Take 2 parts of lemon oil and 1 part of vinegar to make a mix, and go in with a little piece of tissue or sponge in a bowl to wipe stains from the wall.

490. Stack your magazine and newspapers vertically to make them orderly and to create room for many more.

491. You can also make a modest holder with old cereal boxes and cover it with a few colorful magazine sheets.

492. Organize your souvenirs and other display items by putting them in a glass cabinet. It will look great and will make it easier to clean and stop it from getting damaged.

493. Make fancy DIY covers out of soft fabrics like cotton to cover your carpets and couches.

494. The most aesthetic and pleasing setting to arrange your living room is to have your furniture in a way that the carpets surround the couches on three sides pointing toward the TV.

495. Take out all your clothes from your closet and then vacuum them. Make a mix of 2 parts dish liquid and a part of vinegar and go in with a sponge and use it to clean the insides.

496. You can leave your shower gel ajar in your closet so that the fragrance can sip out in bits to keep the place fresh.

497.   You can leave your bar soap open under your pile of clothes to keep your room fresh.

498.   Get rid of mold by placing dryer sheets under your clothes. This way the moisture will be absorbed in the clothes and the building won't have molds.

499.   Roll a piece of double-sided tape around a stick and roll it around the drawer to remove dust and dirt from the drawers.

500.   Use your dry sponge to tackle all the dust, then go in with a wet sponge or a sponge dipped in baby oil to take out the dust fully.

501.   Take out or raise your mattress very often to vacuum the bed. This way dust won't gather and insects won't live there.

502.   Make a mixture of baby oil and water to polish your bed, go in with a sponge and wipe through.

503.   Eliminate dampness from your mattress using talcum powder. Sprinkle it over the mattress and let it soak up the wetness and vacuum the powder.

504. Make use of the lemon juice and vodka mix to remove the wet smell from the mattress. Go in with a sponge and wipe properly.

505. Wondered how to get bed wet stains out of your mattress? Sprinkle your mix of baking soda and solid sea salt over the stain and vacuum once absorbed.

506. Take out tiny bits of glass from a surface by making little dough and use it to pick the dirt.

507. Pepsi and Coca-Cola have caffeine in them.

508. Pour some milk over an ink stain on your cloth, and use a slice of fresh lemon to rub it off. Then wipe it off with a wet sponge.

509. Place your sponge in hydrogen peroxide, then use it to wipe off the sweat stains under your armpit or by your collar. The stain will be no more!

510. To quickly wear an unwashed cloth, spray vodka on it sparingly or go in on the cloth with a vodka-wet sponge over the cloth to take out an unpleasant odor.

511. Clean your leather jackets by using closed-grain sandpaper to brush all the dirt and stains away. You can then dip a sponge in baby oil and

polish your jacket. You can also use glass polish to clean your leather jackets.

512. Make a mixture using toothpaste, baking soda, and lemon juice to clean out jewelry.

513. Take out alcohol stains from your clothes by pouring some white wine on top of it and letting them dry out for some minutes. Throw it in the washing machine and wash it.

514. To take out dried chewing gum from your clothes, put some butter paper on it and put a hot iron over it. The gum will melt on the paper.

515. You can also sprinkle salt over it, and place the iron on it. The stain will stick to the salt and then clean the iron afterward.

516. Make a mix of baking soda and vinegar and use a piece of steel wool and wipe off the gum.

517. Place a cup of vinegar and 5 cups of water in a bucket, then soak the baby clothes for close to 30mins and then rinse with water.

518. Use hydrogen peroxide and a little dish of liquid mix to clean out your canvas shoes.

519. For very dirty shoes, soak them in a bucket with a half cup of dish liquid and 5 cups of water.

520.   Pour some vodka and water into a container and put on your socks to stop the foul smell. Put the tissue in your shoes to also suck up the sweat.

521.   To take out the dust and dirt from under your suede shoe, use sandpaper or a nail file. Then polish with body lotion.

522.   Make jewelry hangers from the old hangers you no longer use.

523.   Make use of your old shoe boxes to organize your drawers.

524.   To keep your closet from getting clustered, separate your clothes based on the occasion.

525.   Make a mix of bottled soda and mouthwash, then put it in a bottle and shake well. Pour it over your toilet bowl overnight and flush it the next morning.

526.   To unclog your toilet, drop Alka seltzer tablets in it.

527.   Use a sponge dipped in baby oil to wipe the walls of your toilet to give it a shine.

528.   Make use of pumice stone or sandpaper to scrub rusty parts in the toilet.

529.   Put some vodka in a spray bottle, and spray outside the toilet to hinder the mold from gathering. Wipe off with a sponge.

530.   Unscrew your shower heads and put them in a plastic bag which has vinegar to clean it. Tie the bag with a rubber band.

531.   Mix borax and baking powder and sprinkle around the bathroom to eliminate germs.

532.   Eliminate rusty stains in the bathtub by spraying some vinegar over the stain and scrubbing with the aid of steel wool.

533.   To take out hard stains, spread some coarse sea salt, lemon juice, and citric acid crystals over the stain. Allow to settle, then scrub off with steel wool.

534.   Add some drops of baby oil or mineral oil with water to prevent the tub from having rings.

535.   Cover the surface of your bathroom surrounding with cling film so it doesn't get dirty.

536.   Cover your bath cans with cling film so it doesn't get rusty.

537.   Apply transparent polish beneath your bath cans to hinder them from rusting, or forming marks or stain platforms.

538.   Get a bucket and add 5 cups of hot water, some eucalyptus oil, and some liquid wash and turn. Go in with a mop to wipe the bathroom tiles.

539.   Eliminate tile molds from gathering by using your sea salt and borax mix.

540.   Bees or buzzing insects can be taught to detect bombs

541.   Get lemon juice and borax and mix, then go in with a sponge and scrub the tiles.

542.   Dip your sponge in hydrogen peroxide and wipe your tiles to make them shine.

543.   Mix baking soda and vinegar and go in with a toothbrush to eliminate difficult water stains.

544.   Wipe off fingerprints from taps and faucets using wax paper.

545.   Wipe off rust stains using a sponge dipped in lemon juice, then wipe off.

546.   Make use of newspaper to wipe dirty mirrors from left to right.

547.   Apply a thin coat of shaving cream over tissue to prevent mirrors from getting foggy, then wipe properly.

548.   Clear off scuff marks from your mirror using toothpaste over it, then wipe it off with a wet sponge.

549.   It's best to put your cosmetics and towels in a wicker basket.

550.   Get a new self-made towel or clothes hanger by repurposing your old ladder, have it painted and it looks great!

551.   Worried that you have lost so many pins lately? Attach a magnet inside your cupboard and have your pins stored there.

552.   Tied of using shower curtains? Hang thick ropes instead!

553.   Sprinkle some talcum powder over the oil in your garage and let it soak up. Wait till it congeals and then goes in with your vacuum.

554.   For tough stains, place a little blotting paper over the stain and go in with a hot iron over the stain. The stain will melt on the iron and soak in the paper.

555.   Your garage can be less greasy by wiping it with a mix of warm water and alcohol.

556.   The mix of alcohol and warm water can get eliminate rust and difficult stains.

557.   Use instant coffee powder in a bowl to remove the foul smell from your garage.

558.   Mix some drops of rose essential oil in some water and spray around the garage to keep it smelling fresh.

559.   Add some lemon juice, alcohol, baby oils, and warm water together to mop the floor of your garage to keep it tidy.

560.   Use boxes to organize your garage better. Tag each box so it's easy to identify each item.

561.   Arrange the boxes vertically to make the garage spacious enough.

562.   Don't forget to use a permanent marker to scribble on the boxes, it's more durable.

563.   Hang your tools on the wall of your garage to make it easy to find them.

564.   Rap steel tools in dryer sheets to prevent them from rusting or gathering moisture.

565.   Apply nail polish on tiny scratches on the body of your car to get rid of them.

566.   Place your car cover in a tub of warm water and liquid wash to clean it. Put it under the sun to dry out totally, then cover the car back.

567.   Loosen the ice that forms over your car lock, and rub some hand sanitizer on it.

568.   Get rid of the foggy effects of your car light by placing some whitening toothpaste over it. Place a tissue over the paste and wipe it off.

569.   Mix some drops of essential oil, vodka, and 1 part of olive oil to make a car perfume. Pour the mixture into a little bottle and use a twin side tape to stick it to the dashboard.

570.   Can you believe that there is no gravity in space? The reality is that gravity exists in all areas of space.

571.   Hydrochloric acid is made in our stomach by Parietal cells that's why our food can break down.

572.   There is a time in the Earth's evolution when movement is delayed called 'the boring billion.'

573.   Nikola Tesla, a Scientist drank whiskey daily because he thought it would make him live to 150.

574.   Does the Earth have four moons? Duncan Waldron discovered asteroids close to the sun in 1986 that look like the earth, so we don't have four moons.

575.   With the aid of magnetic fields in microgravity, rabbit, beef, and fish tissues were produced on the International Space Station by a Russian 3D bioprinter.

576.   Minus 40 degrees Celsius is just the same as minus 40 degrees Fahrenheit.

577.   Space perspective has started selling seats for luxurious balloon rides to space in 2024 worth $125,000 for each person.

578.   Gary Schwartz experimented if there is life after death and called his book — The Afterlife Experiment where his findings can be found.

579.   Pooter is a device used by entomologists to pick up live insects.

580.   The Milky Way is about 100 thousand to 120 thousand light-years in diameter.

581.   Artist Max Siedentopf is making a connection called "Toto Forever" at a secret site somewhere in the Namib Desert, Africa.

582.   Mantra rays are the fish with the biggest brain, they can identify themselves in from of the mirror and can be self-aware.

SCIENTISTS THAT DIED OR GOT INJURED BY THEIR EXPERIMENTS

583.   Karl Scheele discovered oxygen, tungsten, chlorine, molybdenum, manganese, and a process close to pasteurization. Scheele died from tasting his inventions (mercury poisoning).

584.   Jean-Francois took the initial manned free flight in a hot air balloon at an altitude of 3000 feet. He died at fifteen hundred feet in a hot air and gas balloon. The balloon deflated and he fell to his death.

585.   David Brewster founded the toy — kaleidoscope and majored in optics & light polarization inquiring about exceptional vision. His chemical experiment done in 1831 almost blinded him. He battled eye challenges till death.

586.   Elizabeth Fleischman Ascheim participated in studies about electrical science. She bought an x-ray machine and made herself a subject. She died of bad cancer after much radiation exposure.

587.   Scientists estimate there are 400,000 species of plants on Earth and more than half of them are thought to be edible.

588.   The taste modifier in the Miracle Berry or synsepalum dulcificum has Miraculin which is responsible for altering the taste buds.

589.   Alexander Bogdanov died after his blood attacked him. He experimented with blood transfusion, in 1928 he transfused blood from malaria and tuberculosis-infected.

590.   Robert Bunsen blinded himself in one of his eyes. He nearly died once from arsenic poisoning. After this, he lost the use of his right eye after cacodyl cyanide exploded on him.

591.   Sir Humphrey Davy, was a British chemist who caused many explosions and was laid off from the apothecary he worked in. Due to his habitual inhaling of different gases, he was rendered invalid till he finally passed.

592.   The electric chair was invented by a dentist named Southwick.

593.   Michael Faraday was Sir Humphrey Davy's apprentice. Faraday improved on Davy's techniques of electrolysis and electromagnetics. Faraday suffered a nitrogen explosion, got blind, and died from chronic chemical poisoning.

594.   Alf Adams the British Physicist came up with the idea of the 'strained-layer quantum well laser' walking on the beach with his wife.

595.   Marie Curie and her husband discovered radium. She performed a lot of radiation research for radiation therapy. She was exposed so much to radiation that and contracted leukemia and died in 1934.

596.   Marie Curie is the first and only individual to bag two Nobel Prizes in science in chemistry and physics which are two different fields.

597.   Galileo Galilei is referred to as the father of modern physics. He refined the telescope but that research led to the loss of his sight.

598.   There have been many UFO sightings reported of magnetic and electromagnetic disturbances. The UFO detector beeps and flashes in situations like this, warning of an impending alien visit.

599.   Sir William Herschel found Uranus in 1781 and originally named it Georgium Sidus (George's Star) after King George III; his new patron.

600.   Latchkey incontinence is the increased feeling of "having to go" anytime you get closer to

the restroom. It's a conditioned involuntary reaction.

601.   Ever heard the saying that lightning never strikes the same place twice? Well, that's a myth, lightning strikes the same place twice! It's a common occurrence.

602.   German scientist, Gerhard Domagk, established the antibacterial agent Prontosil, a sulfonamide.

603.   In 1993, the Scole experiment occurred in the Norfolk village of Scole, England. Over 500 experiments took place and there were records of solid beings, and luminous spheres flying about during the experiments.

604.   Unbelievable but true – When two pieces of metal touch in space, they are permanently stuck together! It's called "Cold Welding"

605.   A lightning bolt is 54 thousand degrees Fahrenheit. That's scorching than the sun's surface!

606.   Marie Curie was the first female professor at the University of Paris.

607.   Pop star Madonna was fired for squirting jam on a customer while she worked at Dunkin' Donuts.

608.   The first instruments ever made were flutes made of bone and mammoth tusks dating 9000 BC.

609.   Playing Skrillex's 'Scary Monsters and Nice Sprites' lessens mosquito bites and also impedes their capacity to mate.

610.   There is a band named 'NǽnøĉÿbbŒrğ Vbёřřʜōlökäävs₮' (pronounced 'Nanocyborg Uberholocaust') initiated from Antarctica.

611.   Shakira was expelled from her school choir since her music teacher didn't think she can sing and she sounded like a goat.

612.   The band Foo Fighters began with only Dave Grohl playing all the instruments and singing all the vocals.

613.   Guitarist Slash of Guns N' Roses once bumped in on his mother naked in bed with David Bowie.

614.   Shaggy served as a US Marine in Operation Desert Storm in the First Persian Gulf War.

615.   The Alexander Piano was the world's largest grand piano built by 16-year-old Adrian Mann. It weighed ~1.2 tons and was almost 19 feet long.

616.   The kaisatsuko is a fiddle-like instrument invented by Yuichi Onoue in Tokyo, Japan, It uses a hand crank that turns a nylon wheel, bending the strings and making a sustained drone sound.

617.   The hurdy-gurdy also uses a rotating wheel to bend the strings technique. It was invented before the 11th century.

618.   Trixie Trang in Fairly Odd Parents and Kimi in Rugrats was voiced by actress Dionne Quan, she is officially blind and all her acting scripts are written in braille.

619.   The world's longest album title was written by the band Chumbawamba at 156 words and 857 characters long for the 2008 album.

620.   A musical saw is using a regular handsaw bent into an S-shape as a musical instrument.

621.   Lady Gaga was bullied by her classmates at NYU. They made a Facebook group named "Stefani Germanotta, you will never be famous"

622.   Judy Garland is popular for her character in 1939 as Dorothy Gale in the MGM classic film The Wizard of Oz.

623.   "Over the Rainbow" has been voted a top movie song of all time in the American Film Institute's 100 Years 100 Songs list.

624.   Miley Cyrus's earliest job was to pick up the bras and the underwear that her dad's fans (country singer Billy Ray) flung on the stage.

625.   I bet you didn't know that Michael Jackson was the youngest child singer turned "King of Pop".

626.   British Academy of Sound Therapy revealed that the song Weightless by the Marconi Union is the most relaxing ever.

627.   Grammy award-winning Jamaican rapper Shaggy was famous for his hits "It Wasn't Me" and "Boombastic."

628.   The guy who wrote "Louie, Louie" sold the song's rights for $750 to pay for his wedding in 1959.

629.   Michael Jackson was projected as an eleven-year-old instead of nine so he looks charming and friendlier to the media.

630. The bazantar is a five-string acoustic bass, fortified with an extra twenty-nine sympathetic, and four drone strings beneath the top five original bass strings.

631. The bazantar spans over five melodic octave ranges, and the sympathetic section holds four more octaves.

632. Grindcore was created by Napalm Death. He belonged to a metal band.

633. The popular "Father of Death Metal" is said to be the late guitarist Chuck Schuldiner.

634. Slayer is one of the big four that created thrash metal alongside Metallica, Anthrax, and Megadeth.

635. Manowar is power metal, mostly singing of fantasy and looking the part of the warriors they say they are.

636. A popular and influential gothic metal band is Celtic Frost.

637. Venom a black metal band projected Satan in their music and that made them more famous.

638. Motorhead by Lemmy and his great vocals and crazy bass were insane.

639.   Iron maiden – The NWOBHM (New Wave of British Heavy Metal) has the greatest impact and was the beginning of metal.

640.   Iron maiden opened up the path to catchy, wailing vocals, strong lyrics, and notable songs.

641.   Judas Priest released some timeless classics such as "Breaking the Law" etc.

642.   Black Sabbath was the very first metal band. They opened the world up to the true beauty of metal music.

643.   The cimbalom is a kind of hammered dulcimer, with strings pulled across a sounding board and also struck with a mallet or plucked to make a sound, it is popular in Romania, Ukraine, Greece, Hungary, etc.

644.   The Cimbalom was made popular by Zoltán Kodály in his orchestral suite – Háry János.

645.   The Cimbalom was used recently in the film – The Lord of The Rings: The Two Towers to highlight Gollum's sneakiness.

646.   Daniel Johnston became popular after the Devil and Daniel Johnston documentary. Daniel battles with mental illness and his songs show

childlike marvel and hope, mixed with darker themes.

647.   The contrabassoon is the most uncommon orchestra instrument which is almost twice as long as a standard bassoon.

648.   It takes so much more breath to play than a bassoon, and the deepest note can make the room you're in vibrate!

649.   The stalacpipe organ is the largest musical instrument in the world kept inside the Luray Caverns in Virginia's Shenandoah Valley.

650.   The oldest known musical composition to survive in its entirety is a song called the Epitaph of Seikilos.

651.   Buried underground in the middle of downtown Boston lays an abandoned 120-year-old concert hall.

652.   Snoop Dogg arrived 2 hours late to a concert in Haarlem, Netherlands in 2015 and went straight to stream football on his laptop while performing.

653.   Tara Strong, the voice actress for Bubbles from "The Powerpuff Girls" has done 573 other credited voice roles.

STRANGE ANIMAL FACTS

654.   Bees and their mystery... once a swarm of over 20,000 bees once trailed a car for two days since their queen was trapped inside the car.

655.   Every year, U.S. farmers save an estimated $22.9 billion on pesticides because bats eat so much of their insects.

656.   Meet the brave Amazonian parrot named Freddy Krueger who survived being kidnapped, shot, and bitten by a snake. He later found his way back to a Brazilian zoo.

657.   Some animals and insects, similar to squirrels and bumblebees, apply a "mating plug" to stop other males from fertilizing females they have already mated.

658.   UK fisherman, Andy Hackett caught a 70-pound Fanta-colored monster of nature. This ornamental hybrid specie is of koi carp and leather carp. This is the largest ever.

659.   Gibbons begins each day by singing at sunrise.

660.   Cave Swifts make their nests by spitting a chemical substance into the air that hardens.

661. It takes at least eight bees throughout their life to make a single teaspoonful of honey.

662. African grey parrots are very social and recent research confirmed they have developed the gift to act selflessly.

663. The mannerism of African grey parrots is the first-time nonmammals have been noticed assisting each other in this way.

664. Talero, a German shepherd stayed next to the body of his owner for 23 days after he had died in a snowstorm to keep him warm and wade off scavengers.

665. The male priapium fish (Phallostethus cuulong) was named after the ancient Greek fertility deity Priapus.

666. The reason cats and dogs love to lie in the sun is to convert the oily cholesterol on their skin to vitamin D3.

667. The male priapium fish has its genitals right under its chin.

668. Tara, the tabby cat, won the SPCA Los Angeles's annual national Hero Dog Award in 2015 for tackling a dog attacking a child.

669. The daddy long-legs spider is not the most poisonous.

670. The brown recluse and the funnel web spiders are the most poisonous spiders.

671. Some lizards have a noticeable third eye known as a parietal eye, it is an opalescent gray spot on the top of their heads.

672. Due to the translucent third sideways eyelid caused by nictating membrane or haw, ducks can keep their eyes open underwater.

673. All birds have the nictating membrane and also humans have a vestigial remnant called the plica semilunaris.

674. When an ant colony is well structured with resources to spare, then winged ants start to surface.

675. The Opossum is a creature with the ability to neutralize almost all poisons.

676. Sea otters have slack skin over their chest which makes a pouch for them to store rocks and food. The rocks are kept to help them crack open shellfish and clams.

677.   Rats are nonemetic, meaning they can't vomit. No wonder rat poison is so effective.

678.   Scrotum humanum was given for the first dinosaur bone found by Richard Brookes in 1763. It later was recognized as part of the femur of a Megalosaurus.

679.   There are silverfish in the desert that don't need to drink, they can absorb moisture from the air through their anus.

680.   Physically, pigs can't look into the sky.

681.   Octopuses have many neurons in their tentacles such that a severed tentacle can continue reacting to stimuli even after they are no longer connected to the main brain.

682.   The Brookesia Micra chameleon is said to be the world's smallest at just over an inch long. It is seen only on the small island of Nosy Hara.

683.   The eyes of Mantis shrimps' are more advanced than those of humans: they have four times as many color receptors and can see visible, UV, and polarized light.

684.   Hippos love to lick massive crocodiles.

685.   Foxes use the Earth's magnetic field to approximate distances. It works as a 'rangefinder.'

686.   Bottlenose dolphins have the longest memory among non-humans.

687.   There is a group of sea wolves on Vancouver Island that can swim for miles and 90% of their diet is seafood.

688.   The Scatophagus argus, which translates to "spotted feces-eater", this fish is known for its indiscriminate eating habits.

689.   The Sonoran desert toad causes one to hallucinate. The psychedelic frog releases a compound called "DMT" which gets people high.

690.   Cockroaches can live for many weeks without their heads as their brains are set inside their body. They will die because they aren't feeding.

691.   Walter Potter dealt with stuffed animals such as robins, rats, toads, etc. his collection was sold off to an auction buyer in 2003.

692.   A dog's sense of smell is 100,000 times stronger than a human's.

693.   The Kitti's hog-nosed bat in Thailand is the world's tiniest mammal.

694.   Cats have a dominant paw almost the same as how humans have a dominant hand.

695.   A leech has 32 brains and 10 stomachs. They have both male and female organs. In total, they have 18 testicles and 2 ovaries.

696.   Titanoboa was an ancient snake that lived about 60 million years ago. It could grow up to 42 feet long and weigh around 2500 lb.

697.   A fresh study discovered that elephants comfort each other when angry with gentle touches and trunk strokes.

698.   A hippo sleeping underwater mechanically goes to the surface and breathes without waking up and does this every 4 minutes.

699.   The North Island brown kiwi is a flightless, nocturnal bird that lays a single egg that averages 15% of its body size (about 1 lb.)

700.   The North Island brown kiwi is the only bird known to constantly have both a left and right ovary as most birds have only a single ovary.

701.   The grasshopper swarm that invaded Las Vegas, Nevada in 2019 was so bad that it appeared on weather radar.

702.   African spiny mice can shed up to 60% of the skin on their backs to escape predators.

703.   When a bee mates with a queen, its ejaculation is so great that it is loud to the human ear.

704.   An extinct bird called Rodrigues Solitaire had strange knob-like balls on its wings.

705.   The first ever cloned sheep was named after Dolly Parton as "Dolly is derived from a mammary gland cell.

706.   The red-lipped batfish or Galapagos batfish (Ogcocephalus darwini) have frowny faces and giant red lips.

707.   Some baby turtles talk to each other while they are still in their eggs so that they all hatch collectively.

708.   Male giant jewel beetles (Julodimorpha bakewelli) love to mate with beer bottles instead of female jewel beetles because it is colorful and bigger.

709.   The Turritopsis dohrnii aka immortal jellyfish can live forever by changing back into their juvenile polyp state after breeding.

710.   A crocodile can't stick its tongue out.

711.   During hard times, the Rocky Mountain tiger salamander can resort to cannibalism and even seal its gills and grow lungs to live on land.

712.   The Icelandic Phallological Museum has the penises of all mammals on display.

713.   Kenyan farmers are using elephants' natural fears of bees and building "beehive fences" that keep wild elephants from trampling the crops.

714.   Chocolate can kill dogs, it contains theobromine, which affects their heart and nervous system.

715.   There is a sea snail that wears iron-plated armor like a suit.

716.   A group of rats is called a mischief.

717.   A mosquito's proboscis has six needles, two of which have 47 sharp edges to help cut through skin and protective layers to suck your blood.

718.   The Lammergeier/bearded vulture is native to the Mediterranean and popular for dropping bones and tortoises on rocks to break them open.

719.   A big cigarette-smoking, beer-drinking bear named Wojtek was recruited into the Polish army during WWII.

720.   Birds eat up to 550 million tons of insects yearly or as many as 20 quadrillions of individual bugs.

721.   Squirrels were meant to remind city inhabitants of nature and feel "rural peace and calm" in the urban American cities in the mid-1800s.

722.   A mouse's sperm is far larger than an elephant's sperm.

723.   The Hercules beetle makes it one of the strongest animals in the world.

724.   The fruit fly produces the longest sperm known to science.

725.   Camels have three eyelids to guard their eyes against the harsh desert sand.

726.   Polar bears are the only kind of bears that are attracted to women menstruating.

727.   Humpback whales have recovered 30 percent of their population. Their population dropped to 450 in the 1950s.

728. Spiders can get high and build various types of webs while on caffeine, weed, mescaline, and LSD.

729. The wingless midge (or small fly) Belgica Antarctica is 24 inches long and the biggest land animal permanently living in Antarctica.

730. A snail can sleep for three years.

731. Dogs possess an evolutionary trick they use in manipulating human emotions by evolving the right RAOL & LAOM muscles that helps them raise their inner eyebrows.

732. A hammerhead shark was birthed in 2001 at Henry Doorly Zoo in Nebraska with three possible mothers in the same tank.

733. Modern research discovered seals brought Tuberculosis to North & South America and not European explorers.

734. Octopuses make their gardens at the bottommost part of the sea.

735. Sea squirts begin as an egg, grow into a tadpole, then fasten themselves to an object, be it a rock, the ocean floor, etc.

736.   Sperm whales are called so because their heads are filled with large amounts of oily fluid, which whalers thought was sperm.

737.   A baby elephant sucks its trunk for comfort as a baby sucks its thumb.

738.   Sea squirts are the only animal that consumes their brain after fully developed.

739.   The boring billion is a period in the earth's evolution that began 1.7 billion years ago.

740.   A lot of the fruit fly's sensory organ resides in their front legs, when this is taken out, they can mate with both sexes and even other fly species.

741.   The only scorpion residing in Canada is the Northern Scorpion which has 12 eyes that are light-sensitive and can only tell light from dark.

742.   A polar bear named Binky mauled two visitors who jumped into his cage at Anchorage Alaska Zoo. He was sold with a tag – "Send another tourist, this one got away".

743.   Elephants have three times as many neurons as humans.

744.   A Texas woman was arrested for trafficking an endangered "Spider monkey" in a box she lied was just beer.

745.   Unlike the popular belief that elephants are very smart, yes they are but not smarter than humans.

746.   The ancient name for the bear was the term bruin, meaning the brown one, which then segued into a bear.

747.   Galapagos batfish use their fins as feet to walk around the sea floor because they're awful swimmers.

748.   Butterflies taste with their feet.

749.   If Goldfishes are kept in the dark or away from sunlight they will lose their color.

750.   Ants only take rest for about 8 Minutes in 12 hours.

751.   The brain of Dogs' have gotten larger and they have gotten smarter compared to cats mostly because dogs are more social.

752.   In the entire world, termite queens are the insect with the longest lifespan. It can live up to 50 years.

753. Sea snails are the only animals to use iron sulfide as skeletal material.

754. The Hercules beetle weighs just 100 grams and can lift 8 kilograms.

755. Termite queens are used in traditional medicine and serve as a delicacy in some cultures.

756. A jewel caterpillar is a beautiful insect covered in bright colors like gummy candies in a pile.

757. Sloths are the only animals that poop once a week.

758. Rats cannot belch nor do they experience heartburn.

759. Penguins poop so much that it stains the ice and makes it easy for scientists to locate them using satellite imagery.

760. When the Spanish ribbed newt is been attacked, it pushes out its ribs until they puncture through its body, revealing a row of bones that act like poisonous barbs.

761. Every polar bear is left-handed.

762. Research has it that migrating humpback whales can be linked to their original region by their whale songs.

763. Gray whales' mating ritual consists of a third "male escort" whale courting the female.

764. Every origin and population of whales has its unique songs.

765. Sperm whales are the loudest animals on earth as their volume reaches up to 230 decibels.

766. The loudest animal's voice which is Sperm whale is twice as loud as a jet that is taking off.

767. Unfertilized ant eggs often produce male ants and fertilized eggs make female ants, thus all male ants are fatherless.

768. Squirrels are tricksters! Most times they pretend to be digging the ground to bury their spare nuts, but they are faking it.

769. Slugs have approximately 27,000 teeth. They normally get weary and fall off, but they are replaced by moving their back rows of teeth forward.

770. Snapping turtles don't have teeth with their sharp beak and firm jaws but they can make 1000 PSI bite force.

771.   Bees don't often die when they sting. They die when they sting a human or other animal with similarly thick skin.

772.   Sea otters hold hands so they don't drift apart.

773.   The adult Luna Moth doesn't have a mouth and dies of starvation.

774.   The only animals that can't jump are Elephants.

775.   Today ripe watermelons can be detected by an iPhone app. Just knock on the fruit repeatedly with the phone's microphone and a result is given.

776.   A 2015 study by Clear Labs discovered that 2% of the vegetarian hot dogs sold in the US contained human DNA.

777.   The American singer Aretha Franklin always asked to be paid cash upfront before any performance.

778.   Later in the future, we can use close to 30 nights on the International Space Station for $35,000 each night.

779.   The Egyptian Blue color glows under fluorescent lights letting historians recognize the color even when it's not visible.

780.   During the US prohibition era, moonshiners wore cow shoes.

781.   The US Center for Disease Control has a Center for Alertness and Response which comprises specific guidance for zombie readiness.

782.	In 2008, a beach was stolen in Jamaica. Almost 500 truckloads of sand remain missing to date

783.	Santa Claus was invented by Coca-Cola.

784.	Chocolate was formerly consumed in a powder or drink form.

785.	Tree Shaping is growing trees and roots into bridges, fences, chairs, ladders, jungle gyms, tunnels, etc.

786.	Vatican City is the highest crime rate per capita where a minimum of 600 crimes are committed per year, despite only having 800 residents.

787.	In 2016 when Prince died, he didn't leave behind a will for his estate worth hundreds of millions of dollars. To date, it's still not settled.

788.	Queen Elizabeth does not own a passport, all British passports are issued in the queen's name.

789.	Sharon Lopatka volunteered to be tortured and killed in 1996.

790.	Traditional 'high-wheeler' bicycles were also called 'penny farthings.'

791.   Scientists approximate there are 400,000 species of plants on Earth and over half of them are believed to be edible.

792.   Halloumi is special because it doesn't melt due to the manner it was formed. Its curd is heated before putting it in the brine.

793.   A 2015 study in the UK discovered that 72% of 18 to 25-year-olds communicate their emotions better with emojis rather than in words.

794.   A 2011 study discovered that there is a genetic mutation in half the world's population which causes Brussels sprouts to taste very bitter to them.

795.   The Australian Rainbow Lorikeet usually gets drunk on the fermented crimson flower nectar gotten from the Weeping Boer-bean tree.

796.   In 1827, Guinness started selling in Nigeria.

797.   Two actors have accidentally hung themselves for real while playing Judas in live Biblical plays.

798.   In 18th century England, Pineapples were such a status symbol often rented for the evening to take to a party.

799.   Amazon Founder, Jeff Bezos pledged to give away most of his $124BN fortune to fight climate change.

800.   In 1985, when Coca-Cola declared the return of Coke's original formula, ABC News interrupted General Hospital to break the story.

801.   F1 driver named Sergio Perez has memorized the racing track down to the latter.

802.   A sniffer dog discovers £1.2m worth of cocaine hidden in a wheelchair at the Milan Airport

803.   The Desert Bus video game was created in 1995 by Penn & Teller.

804.   Levers are the official door handle in the city of Vancouver in place of doorknobs.

805.   Beluga caviar (fish roe eggs) costs about 5,000 dollars per kilogram.

806.   Keanu Reeves has a private cancer foundation to help children's hospitals and cancer research.

807.   Study shows that Asian men are less attractive than men of other races.

808.   The United States has the oldest and shortest written Constitution of any major government in the world, at 4400 words.

809.   Buzz Aldrin successfully calculated the docking trajectory of the failed NASA Gemini XII flight, with the aid of a sextant and a slide rule.

810.   Until 2008, the chemical TBT was employed in ship's anti-fouling paint, which made female snails develop penises and finally explode because they couldn't shed their eggs.

811.   Change your body language and act more alpha and your testosterone and cortisol levels will change.

812.   In a day, blood travels a total of ~12,000 miles - that's nearly half the circumference of Earth.

813.   In 1971, Saddam Hussein imported 100,000 tons of grain preserved with fungicidal mercury.

814.   2 years were spent cleaning up over 11,500,000 pounds of trash along Mumbai's Versova beach in one of 'the world's largest beach cleanups.

815.   There is just one single-stop sign in Paris, France, located in the 16th arrondissement.

816.   Climate change is making the world's oldest mummies into black goo.

817.   Ronald Reagan left a warning sign for them to beware of George H.W. Bush's dog due to his love for the White House's squirrel population.

818.   Francis Pegahmagabow is the most skilled marksman in WWI. He killed 378 enemies with his Ross rifle and seized another 300.

819.   Neil Armstrong carried with him a piece of cloth and wood from the original 1903 Wright Flyer.

820.   A US study discovered that the more money made, the less time you spend on the internet.

821.   The level of wealth you acquire largely predicts the type of websites visited.

822.   Alaska has an unoccupied Aleutian Island called Semisopochnoi which sits 10 miles east of the 180th meridian.

823.   A tree in La Jolla inspired Dr. Seuss's Trufulla trees in his book – The Lorax.

824.   The 100-year-old Monterey Cypress unexpectedly fell over in June 2019.

825.   In 2015, horse breeder Christina Patino gifted the Queen of England a gift of £5,000 worth of stud sperm for her birthday.

826.   Neophobic people hate anything that has to do with changing routine habits which then results in anger and frustration.

827.   The names of all the continents end with the same letter with which they start.

828.   Scientists discovered that the price paid for a thing influences the way we taste and enjoy it.

829.   The first solid chocolate bar was produced in the 1840s.

830.   Wearing headphones for an hour will raise the bacteria in your ear by 700 times.

831.   The center of the Milky Way smells like Captain Morgan and tastes like raspberries.

832.   In Mexico, a rescue dog named Frida rescued the lives of 12 people who were stuck under rubble due to earthquakes.

833.   The Hygiene standards were so poor that the official 2019 Yu-Gi-Oh competition held by Konami set up a hygiene clause in the rule book.

834.   The first synthetically created color blue was created by Egyptians around 2200 B.C.

835.   A small number of prostitutes in Majengo, a slum in Nairobi, have shown high immunity to AIDS.

836.   Grandmaster Magnus Carlsen is a prolific World Chess Champion.

837.   An estimation of 4 billion people (75% of the earth's population) has no mailing address.

838.   Some orchid seed pods hold over three million seeds inside of them.

839.   An African American named Thomas Jennings invented the dry-cleaning process in 1821 and bought his family out of slavery with his earnings.

840.   The three cosmonauts who died aboard the Soyuz 11 in 1971 are the only 3 human beings that have died outside Earth's atmosphere.

841.   In the US, a check-in does not need to be written on a particular bank check paper.

842.   Bluetooth was named after Harald Bluetooth – the King of Denmark 1000 years ago.

843.   Smallpox now only exists in high-security labs in Russia and the US.

844.   In the 25th amendment, the second part deals exactly with procedures for a President who is not fit to serve.

845.   A lost thumb can be replaced with a toe, the first successful toe-to-thumb transplant was performed in 1964, on a rhesus monkey. In 1972 a human.

846.   The project – eRoadArlanda is a road in Sweden that charges electric cars as they drive on it, it works in the snow and rain.

847.   Harare, Zimbabwe, is one of the most expensive cities since its switch to US Dollars as its currency.

848.   In 2010, Bill Irwin (blind hiker) finished the Appalachian Trail at 2160 miles with the help of his Seeing Eye dog, after falling 5,000 times.

849.   Over 30,000 signatures have signed a petition in support that a seized Russian superyacht called AmoreVero be made a hotel.

850.   Nicotine tea is when a cigarette is infused into brandy or vodka so that its content is

immersed into the drink since it's prohibited from pubs and bars to smoke cigarettes.

851. The first Dialysis machine was made out of sausage casings, beer cans, and a washing machine.

852. Billiard balls began production in 1960 and are made of phenolic resin.

853. The cigarette lighter was invented before the match stick.

854. The majority of the Sahara is made up mostly of rock, rocky plateaus, and gravel-covered plains.

855. The most common mineral found on the earth is quartz.

856. Prince Charles modified his Aston Martin Volante to move on biofuel made from white wine.

857. In Chicago, a man was arrested for giving out marijuana gummy to kids on Halloween because he ran out of candies.

858. Snow fell in the Sahara Desert in 2018.

859. Did you know you can donate your voice to assist individuals with speech impairments so they can select a vocal identity they prefer?

860.   Coca-Cola doesn't exist in Cuba and North Korea.

861.   Ryan Graves the billionaire Uber's first CEO was an unpaid intern at Foursquare, who got hired after he answered a job listing on Twitter.

862.   Umami the first taste is evident in foods like meat, cheese, tomatoes, mushrooms, and more.

863.   The hole in the ozone layer may fully heal by 2080 thanks to the worldwide ban on chlorofluorocarbons.

864.   In 585 BC, a solar eclipse happened in the middle of a battle between the Lydians and the Medes. They promptly ceased fighting and signed a peace treaty.

865.   Organic Day is set-asides to watch as the cows are released to pasture. Somehow, the cows seem to dance away in the fields.

866.   The Oompa-Loompas were at one point known as Whipple-Scrumpets in In Roald Dahl's Charlie and Chocolate Factory.

867.   Glossy magazines are made with a white clay called kaolin making them radioactive.

868.   Oxygen is made in stars. Oxygen is part of the 'ash' that is formed when a star burns.

869.   In 2006, a woman filing for public assistance in Washington failed 4 DNA tests to prove the maternity of her children.

870.   One time, a man sued a dry cleaner's store for $67 million due to the late return of a pair of $1000 pants.

871.   French waiters went on strike in 1907 for the right to have mustaches.

872.   A poll was carried out to exchange the tan color M&M that was unnecessary because of the brown M&M.

873.   A Lyme vaccine convening immunity in 76% of adults and 100% of children was taken off the market after a plea by patient advocacy groups.

874.   Sudan has the most record of pyramids in the world and not Egypt.

875.   Lately, a British Airways Boeing 747 fixed a new sub-sonic record for a flight at New York's JFK and London's Heathrow airports.

876. The chocolate-chip cookie recipe was sold to the Toll House Chocolate Crunch Cookie to Nestlé for a dollar and an endless supply of chocolate.

877. In France before 1907, mustaches were a sign of stature and class, and waiters were perceived to be lower class.

878. Venus flytrap is only found natively within a 60-mile radius of Wilmington, North Carolina.

879. Joseph Stalin had a hidden lab that analyzed the poop of foreign leaders just to build a psychological profile for them.

880. Trees make friends and talk to each other.

881. Daniel Webster ran for president and lost three times, and he turned down the Vice Presidency twice, saying it is a worthless office.

882. The 'new car smell' produces over 200+ chemical compounds leading to the smell we love in cars.

883. Philip Morris persuaded the Czech Republic that smoking was an asset to the country so that people will get to die earlier and the government will millions on hospitals, pensions, and housing for elderly citizens.

884.   More Guinness is consumed in Nigeria, which consumes the second most globally behind only the UK, than in Ireland.

885.   Most lipstick has fish scales.

886.   Watching an eclipse with a bare eye is very dangerous and will harm your vision, it can make you blind.

887.   A surgery named – Trepanation was performed many years ago which involves drilling holes in someone's skull.

888.   The Omeo is a wheelchair created from Segway technology that allows users to travel hands-free at a max speed of 20km per hour.

889.   A Russian geocryologist named Anatoli Brouchkov injected himself with 3.5- a million-year-old strain of bacteria called Bacillus F, just to see what would happen.

890.   The Serbian flight attendant – Vesna Vulović was the only survivor after JAT Flight 367 exploded on January 26, 1972.

891.   When Mussolini was 10, he was expelled from school for stabbing a classmate. He repeated the same thing at his next school.

892.   Creative pencil manufacturers started to color their pencils yellow which is a royal color in China that indicates their high quality.

893.   Angelina Jolie and Brad Pitt sold the rights for the earliest images of their twins to People and Hello!

894.   Peter the Great's "Kunstkammer" was fond of collecting rare and odd things from around the world.

895.   Haribo lost a check for $4.7 million and a kind man returned it, he was gifted 6 bags of Gummy bears.

896.   There are no speed limits in the UK for bicycles, but you can get charged with 'cycling furiously'.

897.   In 1805, morphine was initially isolated from Opium.

898.   According to an article issued in 1918, pink was for boys because it is a tougher color, while subtle blue was reserved for girls.

899.   To date, Walt Disney's body is cryogenically frozen.

900.   The oldest "Your Momma" joke dates back 3,500 years.

901.   The Bluetooth logo is made from the Nordic runes of Harald Bluetooth initials.

902.   A holocaust survivor was cured of Auschwitz's PTSD by LSD which allowed him to sleep for the first time in 30 years without bad dreams.

903.   Powered mouse brains laced with charcoal and bark were used by Ancient Romans as toothpaste.

904.   It's an irony that the horror writer Stephen King must sleep with the lights on.

905.   The word "utopia" means "not a place".

906.   Uranus is the coldest planet in our solar system.

907.   A schoolbook was the bestselling book of Edgar Allan Poe as a living author.

908.   Andre Geim won the satirical Ig Nobel Prize in 2000 for his work on using magnetism to levitate a frog.

909. The word "rainbow" in Latin is arcus iris or arcus pluvius, which pretty much means a "rainy arch".

910. Colombia's brightest rainbow is in its river called the "River of Five Colors".

911. In 2022, the city council of San Luis Potosi in Mexico put their bus driver on bicycles to show them how frightening it is for cyclists.

912. At a Japanese bank, an inexperienced trader tried to sell 1 share of J-Com stock for ¥610,000. He accidentally sold 610,000 shares for ¥1 each in 2005.

913. Herpes can protect you against the Bubonic Plague.

914. Technophobia is the fear of new technology.

915. Women are best at discerning shades of colors, but men are best at tracing fast-moving objects.

916. The "sixth sick sheik's sixth sheep's sick" is believed to be the hardest tongue twister in the English language.

917. 98% of Antarctica is covered by ice that is 1 mile thick.

918.   Samuel Morse was in New York and received a letter that warned of his wife's sickness. He left for home but arrived, but his wife was already buried.

919.   Old NYC subway cars are put in the Atlantic Ocean to help form an artificial reef to function as a habitat for marine life.

920.   Allura red AC is common in candy and soft drinks.

921.   The word 'Homeboy' goes back to the 1800s and was used by African-Americans to refer to each other as people from 'back home.

922.   In the 70s, a "safer cigarette" – The XA Project was established but tobacco companies did everything to bury it.

923.   Miniature cows and bulls can be bought for pets, and they only grow to 1m in height

924.   The portrait of the Queen of England has been on enough international money to make a reformist timeline of her aging.

925.   After the fall of the Roman Empire, the technology to make concrete was lost for 1000 years.

926.   Urban Outfitters sold a board game called Ghettopoly with a bonus.

927.   The Wright Brothers detested the first director of the Smithsonian Institution, who was said to have flown before them.

928.   An acersecomic is someone who has never had a haircut in their life.

929.   Thunder is just the sound lightning makes.

930.   Sand from the Sahara is carried by the wind to the Amazon, renewing its minerals.

931.   Canadian research has it that one-fifth of two-year-olds are good are lying.

932.   To improve hospital design for children, scientists sampled 250 children about their opinions on clowns.

933.   Blondie the lovebird suffered from PBFB (Psittacine Beak and Feather Disease) and shows signs of depression and passes on quicker.

934.   Alaska is both the Westernmost and Easternmost point of the United States.

935.   More than 2,500 of the 3,250 crosswalk buttons in New York City function essentially as mechanical placebos.

936.   Plastic surgery comes from the Greek word "plastike" which means "the art of modeling" of malleable flesh.

937.   The city of Athens's first written laws were written by an Athenian lawyer named Draco.

938.   Like fingerprints, everybody's tongue print is different.

939.   The Cosmic Crisp Apple is to stay fresh for 10 months in a fridge still upholding its deliciously sweet and tangy flavor.

940.   Leonardo da Vinci's idea of contact lenses in his 1508 Codex of the eye, was entirely unfeasible.

941.   Ambergris is a popular additive to several perfumes and it's gotten from the sperm whales' intestines.

942.   There are over 40 million prostitutes in the world and over a million in the USA.

943.   70% of England's land is still owned by 1% of the population, mostly descended from William the Conqueror's army.

944.   The Sahara Desert was formerly a tropical rainforest.

945.   The FBI will reward $10,000 to those who report persons who shoot lasers at planes.

946.   Even though Winnipeg is the coldest city in Canada, it is the Slurpee capital of the world.

947.   Hitler's plan for Moscow was to kill all residents and put a lake in its place.

948.   Noah Webster, the originator of Merriam-Webster, learned 26 languages to evaluate the etymology of words.

949.   Anne Miller was diagnosed with blood poisoning on March 14, 1942, and she was given a tablespoon of penicillin, which was one-half of the entire stockpile of the antibiotic in the whole of the U.S.

950.   Elmer Fudd originally just wanted to shoot Bugs Bunny with a camera. But Bugs drove him insane, making him jump into a lake and almost drown.

951.   The Andromeda Galaxy is the largest in the Local Cluster.

952.   The "Sailors' Handshake" is an exceptional handshake that can perceive if a possible partner has Syphilis.

953.   The Soviets made a prototype laser pistol for their astronauts to use.

954.   In 1992, a Calvin and Hobbes comic referred to the start of the universe called the "Horrendous Space Kablooie."

955.   Yoda's race, and his hometown, were never mentioned in any book, film, or media.

956.   The word "hangover" originally meant "unfinished business", later in 1904, it was a term related to alcohol.

957.   The Mall of America in Minnesota has no central heating. Instead, it is heated by store electronics, solar windows, and body heat from shoppers.

958.   Male survivors of the Ebola Virus Disease can hold the active virus in their sperm, and convey the disease sexually months after their recovery.

959.   London's bus drivers had straps attached to their arms in the 1840s that alerts them when they intend to alight.

960.   Billiard balls' major producer and exporter in the world is Belgium.

961.   The moment you are hesitating trying to recall one's name while introducing that person is called Tartle. It's an old Scottish word.

962.   A 2015 study shows that black coffee lovers are likely going to be psychopaths.

963.   Pepperidge Farms yields above 140 billion goldfish crackers yearly and almost 560 million Milano cookies.

964.   Astronauts in space have to sleep close to fans so that there isn't a CO2 cloud in front of their faces when they exhale so they don't suffocate.

965.   The Cuban dictator, Fidel Castro, died at the age of 90 and had slept with 35,000 women.

966.   The Sahara desert fertilizes the rainforest.

967.   The Mexican Constitution of 1917 was the initial document in history that said every person has the right to an education.

968.   In the past, Walt Disney World had its airport with a singing runway called Lake Buena Vista STOLport runway.

969.   Roy Plunkett mistakenly invented the non-stick coating called polytetrafluoroethylene or Teflon, in a bid to make a new refrigerant.

970.   India's Election Commission sets up a polling station 25 miles inside the remote lion sanctuary of Gir Forest National Park to make the priest of a local temple vote.

971.   In 1959, a Volvo engineer invented and patented the three-point seatbelt.

972.   Jupiter has the shortest day of all eight planets in our solar system.

973.   Cocktails became famous during Prohibition because juices aimed to hide the taste of some of the ingredients in the moonshine like rotten meat, dead rats, wood tar, and others.

974.   Macchu Pichu is an earthquake-proof city in the world.

975.   In 1906, over 800 people attempted to correctly guess the weight of an ox at a fair.

976.   A popular case of Fibrodysplasia ossificans progressive is Harry Eastlack.

977.   Some plants, like the Arabidopsis plant, emit toxins as a defense mechanism.

978. Male human beings produce 1,000,000,000,000,000,000,000,000 times more sperm than females produce eggs.

979. When the moon is directly above your head, you weigh a little less.

980. In 1971, John List killed his entire family, he was caught in 1989.

981. An aquatic biologist named Tim Wong repopulated the rare California Pipevine Swallowtail butterfly species from his backyard!

982. Magician Harry Houdini took a year off from his performance career during WWI to promote the war effort including teaching soldiers how to get out of handcuffs.

983. The woman who initiated Mother's Day later attempted to stop it in 1920 because it had become too commercialized.

984. Moon was Buzz Aldrin's mother's maiden name.

985. The Mona Lisa has no eyebrows.

986.   The man who created the modern American flag Robert Heft did so for a high school project and he received a B- for it.

987.   Research has it that almost half of all US food made is wasted due to unrealistic "cosmetic food" standards.

988.   Der Sternewirth is a time-honored tradition where brewery employees are allowed all the free beer they wish while working.

989.   Leonardo da Vinci wrote backward, not for privacy, but because he was left-handed.

990.   It takes an hour or less to form a cloud.

991.   Roald Dahl, Children's author was given a 'Viking funeral' and buried with pencils, snooker cues, wine, and a power saw.

992.   Microplastics are harmful to marine life, its chemicals disrupt the hormones of the animal.

993.   Colorado interchanged mile marker "420" to "419.99" so it won't be stolen.

994.   Only 5 countries in the world use Fahrenheit to measure temperature.

995.   Recycling just one ton of paper saves 7000 gallons of water, 17 mature trees, 3.3 cubic yards of landfill space, and 682.5 gallons of oil.

996.   Amazon River is the second longest river in the world and it has no bridges over it.

997.   In Sweden, you can order Macs on skis.

998.   The Radio show 'Adventures of Superman' exposed the 'secret' codes and rituals of the KKK. It made the KKK a laughingstock and negatively affected their recruitment thereafter.

999.   The drunkard's cloak was the punishment that was used in the UK, Netherlands, USA, and Denmark.

1000.   In Shampoo and Moisturizer Ads, "Essential Oils" means that the oil gives off a unique scent, not that they're essential.

1001.   Elon Musk invested all of US$180 million and then had to borrow money in 2008 from friends to pay his rent.

1002.   The Mont Blanc is on display in the Teyler's museum in the Netherlands.

1003. The drooping ear is a feature for domesticated animals that hardly occurs in the wild (elephants are an exception).

1004. It is possible to walk from Russia to Alaska on ice.

1005. In 2013, the United States exceeded Russia and Saudi Arabia and today makes more oil and natural gas than any other nation in the world.

1006. The 6 quarts of blood in the human body circulates through the body three times every minute.

1007. Women blink almost twice as much as men!

1008. The Philippines accounts for 43% of the world's gin consumption.

1009. Queen Isabella of Spain was the first woman to appear on a US postage stamp to honor her patronage of Christopher Columbus's voyage.

1010. The American Zoo Association has had a "matchmaking site" called the Population Management Center since June 2000.

1011. Shine a black light on a person with Vitiligo and their skin will glow green, yellow, or blue.

1012. There exist a specie of orchid that appears like a monkey's face called 'Dracula Simia'.

1013. A Russian single mother birthed 69 kids.

1014. Thomas Jefferson served mac and cheese at dinner to his guests when he was president and improved on it by making his recipe.

1015. The Toronto Maple Leafs are not titled the Maple "Leaves" because the name was selected in honor of the Maple Leaf Regiment from WWI.

1016. We are all made of stars. The elements in our bodies come from the thousands of stars in our Milky Way.

1017. The vending machines in Japan dispense drinking water for free even if the water supply gets cut off in a disaster.

1018. Coffee was very key in Turkish culture and under 15th-century law, a woman can divorce her spouse if he doesn't provide her with enough coffee.

1019. The South African Big Baobab Tree Bar was 155-foot-wide.

1020. Carl Panzram suffered years of sexual abuse, torture, and beatings.

1021. There are very violent and dark dust storms on Mars.

1022. Fireworks were illegal in Florida since 1941, except for farmers to scare birds from the crops.

1023. In 1964, George RR Martin purchased the first ticket to the first Comic Con.

1024. "Butt" was a medieval unit of measure for wine.

1025. Due to alterations in local gravity, a pendulum clock correct at sea level will lose about 16 seconds per day if relocated to an altitude of 4000 feet.

1026. In 1961, when the Six Flags over Texas theme park began, it had a section devoted to the Confederacy that had actors hunting through the crowd for Union "spies" and "executing" them by firing squad.

1027. You can drink and drive only in Mississippi as long as your blood alcohol content level is below the legal limit.

1028. Isaac Newton's work led to 28 convictions, one being hanged for high treason.

1029.   In the Netherlands, there is a village with no streets, only canals.

1030.   The letter 'E' was used to label a failing grade till it was phased out by the 1930s over the fear of students interpreting it to mean 'excellent'.

1031.   In 2017, France passed a 'right to disconnect law letting people disregard emails that arrive outside business hours.

1032.   Wellington boots were designed by Germans, named the Irish, manmade by an American in France, and first worn by French laborers.

1033.   Almost one-third of the Earth's land surface is concealed by deserts or partial deserts.

1034.   China has just a one-time zone.

1035.   Malta is the shortest nation in Europe.

1036.   A terminal cancer patient was given a worthless drug that caused his tumors to "melt like snowballs on a hot stove in 1957.

1037.   At 16, Seth Rogen paid the bills and was the key wage earner of the family.

1038.   "Bless you" is appropriate when you sneeze because your heart stops for a millisecond when you sneeze.

1039.   Mark Twain an American author, repaid his pre-bankruptcy creditors in full, though he had no legal obligation to do so.

1040.   Study says that close to 50% of the Asian population lacks a particular enzyme found in the liver to absorb alcohol.

1041.   Scientists feel that the Earth may have had two moons at one point in time.

1042.   Before lent and around the New Year, those in Bulgarian kukeri costumes walk with bells and dance around the villages to scare away evil spirits.

1043.   Holographs made by 11 specialized projectors have replaced live animal acts in The Roncalli Circus in Germany.

1044.   Masabumi Hosono is the only Japanese who survived the Titanic, but he lost his job as he was termed a coward for not dying with the other passengers.

1045.   If you remove all the empty spaces between and within the atoms making up every human being, the whole of the human race would fit into the volume of a cube of sugar.

1046.   Blue M&Ms didn't exist until 1995.

1047.   It is impossible to lick your elbow.

1048.   Norway knighted a penguin named Sir Nils Olav III.

1049.   Different potatoes exist in Peru, with over 3800 different types in various shapes, tastes, skins, textures, etc.

1050.   The Antique Vibrator Museum This museum tells us that once upon a time, vibrators were effective tools for the treatment of hysteria in women.

1051.   Abraham Lincoln suffered from depression. He was scared to carry knives so he won't kill himself.

1052.   The human brain is gradually shrinking. We may be getting smarter, but our brains are becoming more compact.

1053.   Japan set up extraordinary concrete tunnels beneath some of their train tracks to permit turtles to cross the tracks.

1054.   Carmine, cochineal extract or natural red 4 has crushed up bugs.

1055.   It was in the 19th century that the word "hangover" was initially showcased in the English vocabulary.

1056.   Only about an estimation of 5% of the population has never experienced a headache.

1057.   The sun is 4.5 billion years old, but it's only at about middle age for stars.

1058.   The odds of being struck by lightning are 1 in 12 thousand.

1059.   "Rhythm" is the lengthiest English word without a vowel.

1060.   A group of unicorns is called a blessing.

1061.   Gold is rarer than diamonds.

1062.   A monkey named Bobby was arrested in 2011 for crossing the border from India to Pakistan.

1063.   Theoretically, a butt load of wine is about 126 gallons or 475 liters.

1064.   The Golden Gate of San Francisco talks.

1065.   Persistence hunting was the earliest form of hunting used to run their prey to death.

1066.   Frane Selak, a Croatian escaped death countless times in the mid-1900s.

1067.   Neolithic people made hundreds of tiny islands, called crannogs. They were erected out of boulders, clay, and timbers about 5,600 years ago.

1068.   The Sahara Desert is made of only 15% sand and dunes.

1069.   The Bahamas, Palau, Belize, the Cayman Islands, and the United States use Fahrenheit to measure temperature.

1070.   The "debate" on vaccines and autism, started after a dishonest paper was published. The author can no longer practice.

1071.   Many girls in China pay $700 for surgery to repair their hymen in advance of their wedding night to fake virginity.

1072.   A theory on why we are ticklish is that it serves as a tool for developing combat skills.

1073.   High heels used to be a necessary accessory for horseback riders and weren't connected with being feminine.

1074. A 2015 study by Clear Labs discovered that 10% of vegetarian hot dogs sold in the US had meat in them.

1075. Over 11% of Americans are sick with parasitic Pinworms.

1076. In the late 1600s, London was afflicted by a sexual attacker, called 'Whipping Tom'.

1077. Finland became the first nation globally to make broadband internet a legal right for every one of its citizens in 2010.

1078. In Modjadjiskloof, a 1700-year-old baobab tree in South Africa held a 15-person full bar in it.

1079. On earth, only two species have domesticated other species – humans and ants.

1080. The Concorde supersonic jet stretched during flight owing to the heat it generated.

1081. Zerão or Estádio Milton Corrêa is a multi-purpose stadium in Northern Brazil.

1082. Did you know that a 2013 study revealed that chewing gum boosts visual memory and concentration?

1083.   Mary, or Maryam in Islam, is cited more often in the Qur'an than she is in the Holy Bible.

1084.   Gold was the most popular investment to ever exist until the stock market came to be.

1085.   There is a unique volcanic rock called pumice that can float in water.

1086.   Cuddling can relieve pain and speed up physical injuries to a huge extent through the release of oxytocin.

1087.   When a shuttle reaches orbit height (around 250 miles above the earth), gravity drops by only 10 percent.

1088.   George Washington's ill-famed wooden teeth were human teeth from slaves.

1089.   Swiss scientific pioneer Horace Bénédict de Saussure take out the top of Mont Blanc at 15,344 ft in 1787.

1090.   If mature cherries are not dried after it rains, they will soak up the water, split, and can't be picked and sold.

1091.   There is a book from the perception of a successful sociopath/psychopath about the intricacies of life called "Confessions of a Sociopath: A Life Spent Hiding in Plain Sight".

1092.   Pencils are typically yellow because the best graphite came from China in the 19th century.

1093.   A crevice and a crevasse aren't the same things.

1094.   The Cosmic Crisp Apple was examined and established for 22 years by WSU's tree fruit breeding program.

1095.   The Queen of the United Kingdom is the legal owner of one-sixth of the Earth.

1096.   Two guys caught the words biggest carp after using their dead friend's ashes as fishing bait.

1097.   In central China, many villagers have used dinosaur bones in medicine and soups, they thought they were from dragons.

1098.   When Michael Bay was a kid, he puts firecrackers on his toy trains and film the results.

1099.   There is a real-life Spirited Away bathhouse exists in Tainan.

1100.   The number of islands in the Philippines is 7,641.

1101.   A "dash" is 1/8 of a teaspoon, a "pinch" is 1/16 of a teaspoon, and a "smidgen" is 1/32 of a teaspoon.

1102.   There's a rock in Australia that's larger than Ayer's Rock Uluru.

1103.   Valentina Vassilyeva a Russian labored 27 times and birthed 16 pairs of twins, 7 sets of triplets, and 4 sets of quadruplets.

1104.   About 80 percent of the world's freshwater originates in the mountains.

1105.   The effect of the asteroid that killed the dinosaurs was great enough to send Earth rocks to Mars and even Europa.

1106.   Studies discovered in Canada that toddlers who begin to lie early aren't likely to do better in life.

1107.   Coca-Cola was formerly green.

1108.   There are waterfalls under the ocean's surface.

1109.   A Norwegian adventurer and scientist named Thor Heyerdahl sailed 5,000 miles across the Pacific in a hand-built raft in 1947.

1110. The Soviet Union hid that a reactor had exploded at Chernobyl until 3 days after when radiation from the disaster set off alarms at a nuclear plant in Sweden 1000 km away.

1111. Did you knowledge that the founder of the fashion and perfume empire Chanel - Coco Chanel was a nazi spy? This was during WWII with the code name of 'Westminster'.

1112. Sometime in 2012, a Georgian designer created a fake Louis Vuitton condom and sold them for $68 per piece.

1113. Astraphobia is the fear of thunder and lightning.

1114. Clinique and Crayola teamed up to make a box of lipstick crayons that are color-matched to actual Crayola shades.

1115. Glitter is bad for the environment. It contains products made from plastic, which adds to the problem of microplastics in our oceans.

1116. The FBI warned Russell Crowe that al-Qaeda was planning to kidnap him as part of a "cultural destabilization plot" In 2001.

1117.   New Zealand owns the steepest residential areas in the world.

1118.   A genetic disease called Fibrodysplasia ossificans progressiva makes human tissue become bone.

1119.   The word "junkie" was coined in the 1920s when drug addicts stole scrap metal to fund their addiction.

1120.   In 1929, a "Bat Tower" was built in the Florida Keys to regulate mosquitos.

1121.   10 Downing Street, the residence of the Prime minister of the UK, has a cat with the government title of Chief Mouser to the Cabinet Office.

1122.   A seven-year-old Indian boy complaining of jaw pain was treated in a local hospital and found to have 526 teeth inside his mouth.

1123.   The Incas used colorful knotted cords named Quipu to record numbers and records such as tax obligations, census data, and storehouse records.

1124.   It was illegal for men to be topless in the US until 1937 – even at the beach.

1125.   After a London man was deprived of consent to construct a building on an empty lot, he applied for a permit for a tank.

1126.   Tom Cruise was in a closet in South Park, as Trey Parker was getting around the legal repercussions of calling him gay openly.

1127.   In all of human history, about 100 billion people have perished.

1128.   The word "Oxymoron" is an oxymoron, "oxy" meaning sharp, and "moron" meaning dull.

1129.   There is a 'Nocebo Effect', which is a negative variant of the 'Placebo Effect.

1130.   As of 2016, there were 870 Chinese-licensed "living Buddhists."

1131.   The word sarcasm is traceable to the Greek verb sarkazein, which originally meant "to tear flesh like a dog."

1132.   From 1998 to 2016, the price of college textbooks increased by 90%.

1133.   The Statue of Liberty's initial concept was titled "Egypt Carrying the Light to Asia" depicting a Muslim peasant woman (fellah) protecting the Suez Canal.

1134.   Researchers discovered that dogs have musical tastes.

1135.   Hotel La Montaña Mágica sits deep within the depths of the private Huilo-Huilo biological reserve in Chile.

1136.   Studies reveal that eliminating lead from gasoline is a major factor that leads to the dip in the violent crime rate in America in the 1990s.

1137.   In Hawaii, you can experience sunny beaches and snowy mountains on the same island.

1138.   In 1999, a Florida man auctioned his kidney on eBay.

1139.   People who work in silence are slower and less proficient than those who listen to music while working.

1140.   Mohammed is the most common name in the world.

1141.   Martin Luther King Jr. was only 39 when he died, but autopsy results showed he had the heart of a 60-year-old due to stress.

1142.   Harvard makes enough money on interest from its legacy that it could offer free tuition to its students and still make a profit on the interest.

1143.   In the 1898 Spanish-American war, a warship was sent by the USA to capture Guam. It fired 13 shots at the harbor fort without getting return fire.

1144.   Since at least 500 B.C.E., no educated person has believed the Earth is flat.

1145.   It snows on Mars and Venus, but the snow on Venus is flakes of metal.

1146.   The Infinite Monkey Theorem posits that monkeys with typewriters and an infinite amount of time could make the entire works of Shakespeare.

1147.   E-bay once tried altering their background from yellow to white but received complaints.

1148.   The only difference between Tylenol Cold and Tylenol Flu is the box.

CONCLUSION

Happy Fact-Finder!

Hey there, Amazing Fact-Finder!

You've just zoomed through a universe of "wow" and landed back here with us. How awesome was that journey? You've discovered secrets of the stars, high-fived with history, and even whispered with whales under the deep blue sea. From the curious crunch of quirky questions to the giggles of game-time trivia, we hope each page tickled your brain and filled your adventure bag with heaps of "did-you-knows."

But don't let the journey end here! Your thoughts are like sparkly gems to us, and we'd love to know which fact made your eyes pop the widest. If you had fun exploring this book as much as we had fun putting it together for you, zip on over to Amazon and drop a review. Share with others which facts made you the master of trivia or just how many times you said, "Whoa, really?"

Your reviews not only help us to make more cool books for you but also tell other curious minds what treasures they can find inside these pages. So, wield your pen like a sword and carve out your thoughts for us to read!Until next time, keep your curiosity cap on and remember, there's always more to learn and laugh about.

Thanks a million for reading, and don't forget—every review on Amazon helps make this book an even bigger bash for brains everywhere!

Happy Fact-Finding!